Spiritual
Transformation

SAINT **SHENOUDA**PRESS

Spiritual
Transformation

by: Viola Yassa

ST SHENOUDA PRESS
SYDNEY, AUSTRALIA
2018

Spiritual Transformation

ST SHENOUDA PRESS
8419 Putty Rd,
Putty, NSW, 2330
Australia

www.stshenoudapress.com

ISBN 13: 978-0-6482814-3-6

CONTENTS

INTRODUCTION 7

SPIRITUAL TRANSFORMATION 11

WORLD-UNCONFORMED BUT

CHRIST-TRANSFORMED 23

A WORSHIPPING COMMUNITY 37

GIFTS OF THE SPIRIT 55

HARMONY IN THE BODY OF CHRIST 85

SERVING THE LORD 99

CHRISTIAN ATTITUDE IN TRIBULATION 109

GENERAL CHRISTIAN PRECEPTS 121

HOW CHRISTIANS RELATE TO NON-CHRISTIANS 125

REPAY NO ONE EVIL FOR EVIL 141

INTRODUCTION

St Paul's Letter to the Romans is his most systematic presentation of the Gospel. He explains human sinfulness and the forgiveness that we have in Christ (Romans 1-8). In Romans 9 and 10, St Paul describes a theological problem: Most Jews are rejecting the Gospel. Not only are they missing out on salvation, it makes other people wonder whether God is faithful to His promises. In chapter 11, St Paul affirms that God has a surprising plan for the people of Israel.

After devoting eleven chapters to heavy-duty theology, St Paul transitions in chapter 12 from doctrine to duty, from creed to conduct, and from belief to behaviour. He says, "In light of what God has done, here is how we should live." In other words, we are to live out our beliefs. It is a chapter of action! St Paul's thesis is: Beliefs should impact behaviour.

St Paul wrote that we should be living sacrifices, transformed in our minds so that we please God and do His will. He also described the attitudes that should characterize believers: humility, service, love and peace. The idea of unfeigned love pervades Romans 12. In some ways this is another "Love Chapter" like 1 Corinthians 13. God's love is certainly a major theme in Romans 12.

SPIRITUAL TRANSFORMATION

PRECEPTS OF THE CHRISTIAN LIFE

"I beseech you therefore, brothers, by the mercies of God, that you present your bodies a living sacrifice, holy, acceptable to God, which is your reasonable service," Rom 12:1.

By this preface St Paul shows that God's glory is the utmost goal of everything we do. In times past the sacrifices were presented before the altar: but now the altar is everywhere. In times past other bodies besides our own were offered, but now our own must be offered. In times past, dead sacrifices were offered, but now we must offer those which have the spirit of life in them. Now they are spiritual.

PRESENTING OURSELVES A LIVING SACRIFICE TO GOD

St Paul begins with the word "therefore", indicating that he is drawing a conclusion. "I beseech you therefore, brothers, by the mercies of God, that you present your bodies a living sacrifice, holy, acceptable to God, which is your reasonable service," Rom12:1. Therefore, He entreated the Romans, as his brethren in Christ, by the mercies of God, to present their bodies as a living sacrifice to Him. This is a powerful appeal. "By the tender mercies of God": It has a reference here to the entire Gospel, to the whole economy of Grace or mercy, delivering us from "the wrath of God" (Rom1:18) and exciting us to all duty.

Devote Ourselves to God

Your bodies: Not merely a periphrasis for "yourselves", but in the strict sense "your bodies", i.e., the very part of you which is apt to be "an occasion of falling". The Apostle takes the two main parts of human nur bodies is not the offering of our bodily looks but our bodily behaviour. In the Bible the body is not significant because of the way it looks, but because of the way it acts. The body is given to us to make visible the beauty of Christ.

We receive from the Lord every day the fruits of His mercy. Let us render ourselves; all we are, all we have, all we can do: and after all, what return is it for such very rich receiving? Since God is giving us mercy, we should submit ourselves to Him.

A living sacrifice: A sacrifice is an offering made to God as an atonement for sin; or any offering made to Him and His service as an expression of thanksgiving or homage. It implies that he who offers it presents it entirely, releases all claim or right to it, and leaves it to be disposed of for the honour of God. In the case of an animal, it was slain, and the blood offered; in the case of any other offering, as the firstfruits, etc., it was set apart to the service of God; and he who offered it released all claim on it, and submitted it to God, to be disposed of at His will.

We are to present ourselves to God as those who are alive from the dead (Rom6:13). Only those "alive from the dead", that is, having appropriated fully their likeness with Him in death, are bidden to present their members

as instruments unto God.   That is, a "living" sacrifice
is not only a contrast to slain sacrifices, but it is also a
"living" sacrifice from the standpoint, ground or position
of "resurrection life" in Christ Jesus, thus linking up with
the identification truths of Romans 6-8.

St Paul at least three times in Romans 6 (verses 13,
16, 19) speaks of presenting our bodies or our members
to God like this, and in every case it is so that our members
- our arms and legs and tongues, eyes and ears and sexual
organs would become instruments of righteousness. So

How is the body to become a sacrifice? Let your eye look upon no evil thing, and it has become a sacrifice; let thy tongue speak nothing filthy, and it has become an offering; let your hand do no lawless deed, and it has become a whole burnt offering. But this is not enough, we must do good works also; let the hand do alms, the mouth bless them that despitefully use us, and the ear find leisure evermore for the hearing of Scripture. For sacrifice can be made only of that which is clean; sacrifice is a first-fruit of other actions.   – John Chrysostom

This is the offering which the apostle entreats the Romans to make: to devote themselves to God, as if they had no longer any claim on themselves; to be disposed of by Him; to suffer and bear all that He might appoint; and to promote His honour in any way which He might command. This is the nature of true religion.

Our Bodies Given to God in Worship

Our bodies are to be given to God in worship as a living and continuous response to God. A literal translation of the last clause of verse 1 says, "this is your reasonable service." In light of what Christ has done for us, giving of ourselves wholly to Him by an act of total consecration is the only reasonable and logical thing to do. Sensible people respond to God's mercy by serving Him. We are set apart for Him, to serve Him — and as we do His will, He is pleased. For the true believer, nothing else makes good sense! It's the logical thing to do! This is how believers worship God (it is a "service"), by giving of themselves totally to Him for His service.

Let every act of your body in living be an act of worship. That is, let every act of your living body be a demonstration that God is your treasure. Let every act of your living body show that Christ is more precious to you than anything else. Let every act of your living body be a death to all that dishonours Christ.

Holy Bodies Belonging to The Lord

Holy, acceptable unto God: The qualification sought for in the Jewish sacrifices was that they were to be unblemished, without spot. In like manner, the Christian's sacrifice must be holy and pure in God's sight, otherwise it cannot be acceptable to Him. If the sacrifice of our bodily life is holy, then it is acceptable to God. So what do these words add? They add God. They make God explicit. They remind us that the reason holiness matters, is because of God. They remind us that all of these words are describing an act of worship — "which is your spiritual worship" — and God is the centre of worship. Just as under the old dispensation the mind expressed its devotion through the ritual of sacrifice, so now under the new dispensation its worship takes the form of a self-dedication; its service consists in holiness of life, temperance, soberness, and chastity. God is not pleased when believers refuse to give Him their all. May there be nothing between our soul and the Saviour.

"Holy" means set apart for God's holy will and service. God's people are "saints", set apart for the service of the King of Kings! Do you see yourself as a holy servant of the Most High God?

So how is it a sacrifice? And practically how do you present your bodies to God as sacrifices? Here are three examples where the body being used as an instrument of righteousness and mercy is called a "sacrifice". In Philippians St Paul says, I "have received from Epaphroditus the gifts you sent, a fragrant offering, a sacrifice acceptable and pleasing to God," Php4:18. Your work and giving and Epaphroditus' bringing this gift to me is a sacrifice of worship to God. It shows God's worth in your heart.

The parable of the chicken and the pig: A farmer once approached a chicken and a pig and asked a heart-searching question: "Will you contribute to a ham and egg breakfast?" For the one it was merely a contribution. For the other it involved an absolute sacrifice!

May Rom12:1 be a constant reminder to every believer that we are not our own because we have been bought with a price (1Co6:19-20). We don't have the right to use our body as we please; we have the duty as love-slaves of Jesus Christ to use our body as He pleases. We are bought by blood and bound by love. We are to present ourselves to God as those who are alive from the dead (Rom6:13). In the light of God's mercy and grace as shown at Calvary, how can we do anything less? The believer is to place himself wholly into the hands of God, even as the believers in Macedonia did, "And this they did, not as we hoped, but first gave their own selves to the Lord" (2Co8:5). We can do this as we remember that our Saviour gave His all for us!

Just as man's failure to worship God led to his downfall (Rom1:20-25), so now true worship is the first expression of mankind's renewal.

"Through (Christ) then let us continually offer up a sacrifice of praise to God, that is, the fruit of lips that acknowledge his name," Heb13:15. When the lips join the heart in praise to God, the body becomes a holy, living sacrifice. "Do not neglect to do good and to share what you have, for such sacrifices are pleasing to God," Heb13:16. When you do good, in Jesus's name, with your mouth or your hands or your presence, your body becomes a holy, living sacrifice of worship. A body becomes a holy sacrifice of worship when it is devoted to God's purposes of righteousness and mercy.

If we display our bodies as a living sacrifice, holy and pleasing to God, He will with heavenly condescension design to see to it that we are rewarded with the same glory as those who have given their bodies up to death for the Lord's sake.
— St Bede

In sum, here's the sequence: God displayed His mercy by sending His Son and vindicating His own righteous in saving sinners. We are lavished with mercy because of Christ. We see that and embrace it (faith) and treasure it (worship). And then we live it out with our bodies so that people see that He's valuable to us. He's constantly shown to be the supremely valuable One to us. And others are drawn to His value. "This is your reasonable service." What does this involve? St Paul explains it in Rom12:2.

"And do not conformed to this world: but be you transformed by the renewing of your mind, that you may prove what is that good, and acceptable, and perfect, will of God," Rom 12:2

WORLD-UNCONFORMED BUT CHRIST-TRANSFORMED

Our standard of behaviour is no longer the society around us. "This world" refers to this age. In 2Co4:4 we learn that Satan is the "god of this world (age)". According to Gal 1:4, Christ gave Himself for our sins, that He might deliver us from this present evil world (age). When we were unsaved we were a part of this evil, Satanic age/ world, but God has delivered us out of it. Demas, who was considered to be a loyal believer in Col 4:14 was later (2Tim4:10) described by St Paul in these tragic words, "For Demas has forsaken me, having loved this present world". ("Present" indicating that it is here now but will not last long; it is very temporal). Finally, in Tts2:12, believers are taught by grace to live godly in this present age. We are in this world, but we are not to live as those who are "of this world" and who are part of this world system which is in opposition to the true and living God.

We Are Not of the World

"Be not conformed": St Paul is saying, "Don't be letting the world squeeze you into its mould!" Don't be moulded by the mannerisms, speech, expressions, styles and habits of this world! Stop assuming an outward expression which is patterned after this world, an expression which does not come from, nor is it representative of what you are in your inner being as a regenerated child of God. It is too easy to have an external conduct that looks good, but an inward life and manner of thinking that is offensive to God.

The world's philosophy is pretty simple: If you want something, go get it (partners, possessions, and power). People are important primarily because of what they can do for you. If they can't do anything for you, don't waste your time on them. Public opinion defines truth; popularity is more important than holiness. Faith and everyday living are unrelated. Live for the moment and don't concern yourself with consequences. You are the centre of your universe; don't let anyone push you around! Our world also screams tolerance (religions are the same; accept and affirm same sex marriage) and truth is not absolute (what's good for you is good for you).

You must not be shaped by these influences. You must fight against the tide of sin, self, and Satan. How much television do you watch in the course of a week? How many movies do you watch in the course of a year? What type of music do you listen to? What magazines, books, and websites

do you read? How much time are you devoting to social networking? Who are your friends? What type of influence do they have on you? What are your hobbies? How do you send your discretionary time?

"But" indicates a strong contrast. God follows this negative command with a strong positive command! Here, we see that God isn't satisfied with an external piety that can be seen only by men, but with who we really are on the inside. We do not just continue doing what we have always done. Rather, we are to change, and this change begins in the mind. It takes conscious effort — thinking about how God's way is different from the world around us.

Even though St Paul is writing to the church, we are a group of individuals. These verses are speaking specifically to you. Will one diseased fish affect the whole tank? Will one mad cow infect the whole herd? Will one person conformed to the world have an effect on our church? Yes! Hence, I dare you to be different. Stand up for Christ. Don't go with the flow; go against the grain. Rebel against the status quo — become a disciple of Christ. Your life will be an adventure. Beliefs should impact behaviour.

Transformed by Grace

"Be transformed": The Greek is metamorphosis (we think of the remarkable transformation of a caterpillar into a butterfly). This word is used in Mt17:2 of our Lord's transformation (popularly called "transfiguration"). The Lord was changed in such a way that His inner glory became visible on the outside (compare Jn1:14). Here and in 2Co3:18 the word is used of the transformation process which takes place in the Christian life as the believer is more and more conformed to the image of Christ (more like Him today than I was yesterday; more like Him tomorrow than I am today). In 2Co3:18 the word is used with reference to the change produced by the Holy Spirit resulting from the believer beholding the glory of the Lord Jesus through His Word and being gradually (from one stage of glory to the next) transformed into the likeness of Christ.

And God said: Let us form man in our image. The Devil says: I will deform man by sin. The World says: We must conform man in our image.

Education says: Let us inform man by knowledge.Society says: We will reform man by culture.   Only Christ says: I will transform man by Grace.

We have already seen in Rom8:29, that God's purpose is to conform us to Christ's image. The present tense (in 2Co3:18) indicates that we are constantly to be transformed. It does not all happen in one day or one month or one year. It's a process which will not end until we are with Christ (1Jn3:2). The verb is in the passive voice (in 2Co3:18), indicating that we do not change or transform ourselves! We must be transformed. It is something that God does in and through us. We are to trust Him and allow Him to do what only He can do.

How will this transformation come about? "By the renewing of your mind". It's a mental process. The believer's mind needs to be saturated with the Word of God so that we might more and more see, think and feel as God does. The heart-cry of the believer: "I want what God wants, no more and no less! I want nothing but God's best! Not my will but Yours be done!" This believer who is being transformed is constantly proving (testing and discovering) what is the will of God, even that good, acceptable (pleasing, well-pleasing) and perfect will of God.

How can we be transformed in our minds?

How then shall we be transformed in this way? How can we make our minds new so that we don't think the way the world thinks but the way God thinks about what is good and bad, helpful and harmful, beautiful and ugly, true and false? Let me point you to four biblical steps:

• Recognize your need for renovation. Recognize that you are in need of a deep renovation of the mind. "Now this I affirm and testify in the Lord, that you must no longer live as the Gentiles do, in the futility of their minds; they are darkened in their understanding, alienated from the life of God because of the ignorance that is in them, due to their hardness of heart," Eph4:17–18. This describes what we are all like apart from this renovation.

The root of our futile thinking goes down deep into the hardness of our heart. Hardness of heart gives rise to blameworthy ignorance, which gives rise to alienation from God, which gives rise to a pervasive darkness of understanding, which gives rise to incredible uses of the human mind in the service of futility. When the heart is out of love with God, the mind knows not what it is for. It stumbles like a genius in the dark along a precipice of destruction. Can you think of anything more tragic and painfully ironic than thousands of brilliant men and women of intellect hearing the final sentence: "Your thinking was futile; I never knew you"! So the first step in the renewal of our minds is to recognize the need for deep renovation of heart and mind.

• **Depend on the Holy Spirit.** The second step to a renewed mind that proves the will of God is to depend on the Holy Spirit. St Paul says to St Titus, "God saved us not because of deeds done by us in righteousness, but in virtue of His own mercy, by the washing of regeneration and renewal in the Holy Spirit," Tts3:5. The renewing agent is the Holy Spirit. We cannot make ourselves new. It is a supernatural divine work of God's Spirit. The main work of the Holy Spirit is to change us into new, holy people who know and love the will of God. So the second step to mental newness is to depend on the Holy Spirit. Humbly rely on Him and not yourself.

• **Pray for spiritual understanding.** Pray for the Spirit to give you spiritual understanding that can prove the will of God. We know that St Paul made this a top priority for his churches because this is what he prays for them again and again. For example, in Php1:9-10, "It is my prayer that your love may abound more and more, with knowledge and all discernment, so that you may approve what is excellent." Love abounding with knowledge and insight is the renewal of the mind that can examine and verify and embrace things that are excellent. And St Paul pursues it by prayer.

To the Colossians he writes, "We have not ceased to pray for you, asking that you may be filled with the knowledge of His will in all spiritual wisdom and understanding," Col 1:9. Do we want to be filled with the knowledge of God's will? Yes. That is our heart's desire! Then, according to St Paul, we need spiritual wisdom and understanding — that is, we need to be renewed in the "spirit of our minds" (Eph4:23). And that is what St Paul prays for "without ceasing". So the third step to a renewed mind is to pray for it. Ask, seek, knock. Will not your Father give the Holy Spirit to those who ask Him (Lk11:13)?

• Focus on the glory of God. The fourth step is to focus your attention on the glory of God. You can see this most clearly in 2Co3:18, "And we all with unveiled face, beholding the glory of the Lord, are being changed into His likeness from one degree of glory to another; for this comes from the Lord who is the Spirit." Beholding the glory of the Lord we are being changed. You become like what you behold. You live like what you look at most. For St Paul, this transformation and renewing of our minds takes place as we behold the face of God, spending time in His glory.

"So we do not lose heart. Though our outer nature is wasting away, our inner nature is being renewed every day. For this slight momentary affliction is preparing for us an eternal weight of glory beyond all comparison, because we look not to the things that are seen but to the things that are unseen. For the things that are seen are transient, but the things that are unseen are eternal," 2Co4:16-18.

"Finally, brethren, whatever things are true, whatever things are noble, whatever things are just, whatever things are pure, whatever things are lovely, whatever things are of good report, if there is any virtue and if there is anything praiseworthy; meditate on these things," Php4:8

"And do be not conformed to this world: but be you transformed by the renewing of your mind, that you may prove what is that good, and acceptable, and perfect, will of God," Rom12:2. The ability to prove what is that good and acceptable and perfect will of God begins with having renewed minds; God's normal pattern for Christian transformation is to work on us from the inside out. We may know what the good and acceptable and perfect will of God is, but we can't prove it in our own lives apart from this inner work of the Holy Spirit.

Our mind is renewed by the practice of wisdom and reflection on the Word of God and the spiritual understanding of His Law. The more one reads the scriptures daily and the greater one's understanding is, the more one is renewed always and every day. — Origen

Daily renewal of the inner person — the person who proves what the will of God is — that renewal comes from looking not at the world with all its fleeting glory, but at the unseen things of eternity which are radiant with the glory of God. Then you will be able to test and approve what God's will is — His good, pleasing and perfect will (Rom12:2). After we stop looking to the world, we will see what God wants, and we will find that His way is better. His instructions are not arbitrary rules just to test our loyalty — they are to help us avoid causing pain for ourselves and for others.

God wants your body and your mind; He wants all of you. Is there anything or anyone that you are withholding from God? Is your marriage and family yielded to Him? Is your vocation His? What about your finances or hobbies? Will you present yourself to Him today and every day hereafter? If you will, your life will never be the same.

A WORSHIPPING COMMUNITY

"For I say, through the grace given to me, to every man that is among you, not to think of himself more highly than he ought to think; but to think soberly, according as God has dealt to every man the measure of faith," Rom 12:3

The word "for" shows that the apostle is about to introduce some additional considerations to enforce what he had just said, or to show how we may evince a mind that is not conformed to the world. In Rom12:2 we learned that we must allow the Spirit of God to transform us into the image and likeness of Christ (compare 2Co3:18). If we are going to be like Christ, then we must be humble (compare Php2:5-8) and this is what St Paul's point is in Rom12:3. "I say": this is St Paul's way of giving a mild, gentle command.

"Through the grace given unto me": St Paul had received Grace (God's undeserved favour) to be an apostle (Rom1:5), and as an apostle he is now writing to these Roman believers and giving them a gentle, loving command concerning humility. St Paul first describes how the Roman Christians are to work together as a worship community.

It is hard to give advice without seeming to assume superiority; it is hard to take it, unless the giver identifies himself with the receiver, and shows that his counsel to others is a law for himself. St Paul does so here, led by the delicate perception which comes from a loving heart, compared with which deliberate 'tact' is cold and clumsy. Through the Grace, through the favour, or in virtue of the favour of the apostolic office, by the authority that is conferred on him to declare the will of God as an apostle, St Paul counsels as the first of the social duties which Christian men owe to one another, a sober and just estimate of themselves. This sober estimate is here regarded as being important chiefly as an aid to right service. It is immediately followed by counsels to the patient and faithful exercise of differing gifts.

Think Correctly About Ourselves

"Not to think more highly than he ought to think": we must think correctly about ourselves, and not be puffed up with an exaggerated and unrealistic idea of our own importance and superiority. We must not have a high, lofty, proud view of ourselves, but we need to have God's view of ourselves (see ourselves as God does). "Soberly": having a sound mind and mental health, sensibly, seriously, to have a balanced and correct estimate of myself, to see myself as God sees me.

Consider Gal 6:3. We think we are something; God says we are nothing! We think we are a big number, but we are actually a zero apart from God. But we must not be discouraged at our own nothingness and lack of importance. The good news is that God in His grace is able to make something out of nothing.

Sometimes when you're feeling important, sometime when your ego's way up; sometime when you take it for granted that you are the prize winning "pup"; sometime when you feel that your absence would leave an unfillable hole, just follow these simple instructions, and see how it humbles your soul. Take a bucket and fill it with water, put your hand in it up to your wrist. Now pull it out fast and the hole that remains is the measure of how you'll be missed. You may splash all you please as you enter, and stir up

*the water galore, but stop and you'll find in a
minute, it's back where it was before.*

The lowly man is the one who has caught a true
glimpse of the High and Lofty One (Is6:1,5; 57:15). The
believer who thinks too highly of himself compares himself
with others and exalts himself above others, as he proudly
thinks himself to be more important than someone else.

What is the alternative in St Paul's mind to thinking
too highly of ourselves? The answer isn't thinking lowly
of ourselves (though that is a good place to start to
come back to now and then). The alternative is to think
"according to the measure of faith that God has assigned".
The alternative to thinking too highly of ourselves (self-
preoccupation, self-infatuation, self-exaltation — the roots
of all sin) is not a different sight in the "mirror, mirror on
the wall". The alternative is turn the mirror into a window
through which we see the glory of Christ.

That's what faith is and does. When faith stands in front
of a mirror, the mirror becomes a window and sees on the
other side the glory of Christ. The decisive alternative to
saying, "I am all," is not to say, "I am nothing," but to say,
"Christ is all." Faith looks to Christ, not self, not even the

new self. In fact, the definition of the new-self is the self that looks to Christ as its Saviour and Lord and Treasure and Joy and Satisfaction.

Recognize God's Gift of Faith

Looking at the broader context of Rom12:3, we notice there is something else given by God. The grace of God is mentioned as a gift to the apostle St Paul in the same verse, and that same grace is mentioned as a gift to all believers in Rom12:6: "We have different gifts, according to the grace given to each of us." So, immediately following his discussion of the measure of faith, St Paul speaks of the gifts of the Spirit: prophesying, serving, teaching, encouraging, giving, leading, and showing mercy. In Rom12:3 St Paul wants the Romans to understand that every believer has a special place in the body of Christ and has a special gift given by God for the benefit of the whole body.

Because each believer receives his measure of faith by God's allotment, we are prevented from thinking of ourselves "more highly" than we ought. Recognizing that our measure of faith comes from God prevents pride and encourages "sober judgment". Each of us should recognize the limits of his or her own gifts. At the same time, we must acknowledge the gifts that others possess and that each believer is divinely placed into Christ as a vital and functioning part of His Spiritual Body (Rom12:4-8; 1Co12:27). No member should consider himself or herself as superior to any other but should instead recognize that God has placed us just where He wants us with the gifts He has chosen for us (1Co12:11).

When we see ourselves as we really are, it is impossible to be given over to pride. Whatever faith we have, has come from God. We should see that even our saving faith is a gift from God, and that we have no basis for pride or a superior opinion of ourselves. We have value only because God chooses to give us value; no one has any reason to boast.

Think about yourself differently than the world thinks. So what is that? Think about yourself in accord with, by the standard of, the measure of faith God has assigned you. Faith is looking away from yourself. So, take stock of yourself by looking away from yourself to another. Christ is all, St Paul says (Col 3:11). So look away from self to Christ. That is so revolutionary. Make the measure of yourself the measure of your seeing and savouring and treasuring Christ. If you want to have significance, embrace Christ as the One who is significant. If you want to have value, embrace Christ as the One who is infinitely valuable. Our worth consists in treasuring the worth of Christ. Rom12:3 tells us the main feature of the renewed mind is the contemplating of all reality in a radically Christ-centred way. Self, what value do you have? Answer: Christ is supremely valuable. St Paul is simply changing the categories on us so that we don't get bogged down in the self-esteem search.

The beauty of the self is its self-forgetfulness in Christ. This is the meaning of Christian humility. It is a kind of self-forgetfulness produced by treasuring Christ. The Christian alternative to thinking too highly of ourselves is mainly to think highly of Christ. Thinking about ourselves will produce pride or despair. And both are forms of unbelief. The Gospel alternative to pride is not mere self-condemnation, but Christ-exaltation. The Christian triumph over pride is faith in Christ. Treasuring Christ — especially the mercy of Christ — above all the praise of men and above all the pleasures of earth, is the triumph of Christian humility.

No Room for Pride

"Think with sober judgment, each according to the measure of faith that God has assigned." In other words, the measure of faith we have is a gift of God. God has assigned it. It is the act of our soul. But our inclination to do that act is a gift of God. "By grace you have been saved through faith. And this is not your own doing; it is the gift of God," Eph2:8.

So now two great grounds of boasting are stripped from the proud human heart. First, the boast that I can save myself or satisfy myself is shattered, and Christ is found by faith to be my all — my Saviour, Lord, Counsellor, Friend, Treasure, Joy. I look away from myself and am satisfied in Him.

Then, second, the other ground of boasting is stripped away also: I discover by the Word — and experience it in my heart — that this faith, this looking away from self to Christ — is a gift. I can't even boast that I was smart enough or wise enough or spiritual enough or godly enough or humble enough to believe in Jesus. No. He was simply kind enough and strong enough to overcome all my resistance. Praise be to his mighty mercy.

God is the great Giver of the gifts, and in His wisdom He distributes the gifts in just the right way. "Every man": each one, each believer (none are left out). There is no gift-less believer (there is no believer without a gift). Every believer has been gifted. This took place at the moment of regeneration. There is no need to seek for a gift. A believer would be foolish to seek and try to get what has already been given to him. There is a need to develop and exercise whatever gifts we have, and this is done by being a healthy believer, abiding in the true Vine who is our Life (Jn15:1-5).

When a person is baptised, God gives him gifts as a new member of the family of God. We receive the gifts according to the measure that God has given us, and we exercise the gifts according to the same measure of faith. "To each one of us grace has been given as Christ apportioned it," Eph4:7. God deals to everyone his portion. Not everyone receives all the gifts, nor is the same gift given to everyone in the same measure. Our sovereign God distributes each gracious gift according to the measure of faith that He has bestowed on us.

"The measure of faith": compare verse 6 ("according to the proportion of faith"). St Paul is not talking about saving faith here (the faith through which we are saved,

Eph2:8), but he is talking about particular and diverse gifts which God has imparted to believers and the faith necessary to exercise those gifts. The gifts cannot be exercised rightly apart from faith and trust in the Saviour. God has given to each a "measure of faith" to use for Him.

His main point is: mercy-dependent, mercy-loving, Christ-treasuring people, saved by the mercy of God, are being renewed in their minds, and the first thing he mentions is: they don't think more highly of themselves than they ought. And now he says: All of you who use your gifts for others, do it with deep humility, knowing that you too are dependent on mercy. That is, do it in proportion to your faith (Rom12:3, 6); do it in childlike reliance on Christ. St Paul puts the emphasis on mercy-loving humility in his list of gifts. The reason is that Christian humility is a self-forgetting happiness in Christ. And this humble happiness in Christ is exactly what unleashes the kind of ministry God values — the spirit and attitudes of ministry, not just its task and function. This humility unleashes the spirit and attitude of ministry that loves people best and exalts Christ best.

Unity and Diversity in the Body of Christ

"For as we have many members in one body, and all members do not have the same function, so we, being many, are one body in Christ, and individually members of one another," Rom 12:4-5

What Rom12:4-5 means is that the church is like a human body with arms and legs and hands and feet and eyes and ears and tongue and nose and neck. Just as it is in the human body, so it is in the body of Christ. There is one body but many members, and the members have differing functions, but they are all members of the same body and they all have an important function. All have a function, all are important, all have a part, but the functions are different. In one respect we are many (many members); but in another respect we are one (one body). We are fellow members of the same body, sharing the same life. The truth of these verses is greatly amplified in 1Co12:12-31. "So we who are many are one body": The church has a unity in diversity the way the human body is one with diverse limbs and organs. The church is a unified whole (one body), yet we are distinct within that one body (individually members); we are unified, but there is not a uniformity in the body of Christ.

> St Paul says not that one person received more and another less of God's gifts but only that they are different. We all have different functions, but the body is one and the same – John Chrysostom

But St Paul goes further than that in what he says about the church as a body. Not only do various members have different functions, they also belong to each other. The point is not merely unity in diversity, but also profound interconnectedness. He says, "So we, who are many, are one body in Christ, and individually members one of another." What does "individually members of one another" mean? It means that our unity is more profound than just belonging to the same body. We belong to each other. The unity of the church is more profound than being part of the same organic whole. It is being part of each other. "Individually members of one another" means that we have duties to each other, according to the way God has blessed us. We err when we neglect either aspect; unity should never be promoted at the expense of individuality, and individuality should never diminish the church's essential unity in Christ; He is our common ground, we are one body in Christ. We belong to one unified organism. And we belong to each other. We are part of one organic whole, and we are part of each other.

Why do we divide and tear to pieces the members of Christ and raise up strife against our own body, and why have we reached such a height of madness as to forget that we are members of one another – St Clement of Rome

Serving Each Other with Our Gifts

Then, St Paul tells us how this profound interconnectedness is supposed to work.

"Having then gifts differing according to the grace that is given to us, let us use them: if prophecy, let us prophesy in proportion to our faith; or ministry, let us use it in our ministering; he who teaches, in teaching; he who exhorts, in exhortation; he who gives, with liberality; he who leads, with diligence; he who shows mercy, with cheerfulness," Rom12:6-8

"Gifts differing": all the members have different (not the same) gifts and different abilities which complement each other. This is illustrated by the members of the human body which have different functions (see 1 Corinthians chapter 12). This is an exhortation to use the gifts God has granted to the individual members of the church. He says that we have gifts that differ according to the grace given to us. In other words, the benefits that flow from one member to another flow in the form of unique gifts

that each member has. Giftedness determines much of the way one member graces another member. My hand serves my wounded shoulder differently from the way my feet serve my shoulder or the way my eyes serve my shoulder. The hand has different gifts than the feet and eyes.

God may grace you with an unusually tender-hearted disposition to show mercy. Or He may grace you with an unusual delight in lavish generosity. Or He may grace you with an unusually forceful or bold bent toward exhortation. Or He may grace you with an extraordinary servant-heart that sees needs and moves toward them the way others move toward food when they are hungry.

The point is that these are the forms or ways or channels through which the individual members bless each other. The Grace of God comes down (vertically, as it were) from God, and we bend it outward through our gifts (horizontally) and extend it to others. Each person should do what he or she does best.

We have different gifts, according to the grace given to each of us. Spiritual gifts are not given on the basis of merit, but rather because of the sovereign choice of God. This idea is related in the very Greek word for spiritual gifts which is "charismata", a gift of grace, a term apparently coined by St Paul to emphasize that the giving of these spiritual gifts was all of grace. Spiritual gifts are given at the discretion of the Holy Spirit. "But one and the same Spirit works all these things, distributing to each one individually as He wills," 1 Co 12:11. Spiritual gifts are basically — not only, but mainly — natural endowments supercharged with the Holy Spirit to effect change by Grace. A spiritual gift transmits Grace. Gifts steward Grace (1Pt4:10).

When the local body of believers is healthy, the life of Christ will be manifested, the unsaved will be convicted and God will be glorified. The best way for us to understand spiritual gifts is to know how we can care for and serve one another to the glory of God. Whether we do that through teaching, feeding, healing, or any other method, we have a responsibility to God and to one another to offer ourselves as servants (2 Co 4:9).

Most Christians are quick to point out the personal benefits we receive with our salvation, but we are a little slower to focus on the responsibilities that come with it. When people speak of spiritual gifts, the focus is often on questions like, "Do you know what your spiritual gift is?" While the knowledge of one's gifting can be beneficial, we often lose sight of God's design in these matters. Yes, the particular gifts of the Spirit are benefits to each believer, but they come with great responsibilities.

GIFTS OF THE SPIRIT

Since they are given by the Spirit of God, they are a part of the new life granted to us in Christ (and may be drastically different from our perceived capabilities or desires prior to salvation). A brief examination of three key texts (Rom12:6-8; 1Co12:4-11; 1Pt4:10-11) will show us God's design regarding His gifts. There are varying opinions regarding the number of spiritual gifts, as well as what the gifts are. Romans 12 lists at least seven, and 1 Corinthians 12 lists nine. There is some overlap in these, and there are certainly indications that God has more that He gives His children.

One of the first things that becomes clear in these passages is the diversity of the gifts. When St Paul listed the gifts in Romans 12, he identified different gifts than what he wrote in 1 Corinthians 12, and when St Peter spoke of them in 1Pt4:10-11, he didn't even bother specifying them. Among the things listed are prophecy, ministry, wisdom, knowledge, faith, healing, teaching, exhorting, giving, ruling, showing mercy, speaking in languages, and interpreting languages. Whatever the specific use of each one was, they each fit together as the parts of the body work together to make a functional whole (Rom12:5).

We can certainly learn of the gifts from these lists,

but if we limit the gifts of the Spirit to those few that were enumerated, we miss the point. In all three passages, we are given a specific purpose of the gifts, and that is where we should direct our attention. In Rom12:8, we are told to use the various gifts according to the character of God and His revealed will... with simplicity...with diligence... with cheerfulness." In 1Co12:25, we are told that these gifts were given "so that there should be no division in the body, but that its parts should have equal concern for each other." In 1Pt4:11, the purpose is "that in all things God may be praised through Our Lord Jesus Christ."

"Proportion of faith": this is an interesting expression from which we get the theological term: "analogy of faith" (sometimes referred to as "analogy of Scripture"). "Analogy of faith" means that Scripture is to be interpreted in light of Scripture and in accord with Scripture. The infallible rule of the interpretation of Scripture is the Scripture itself. Any verse must be understood in light of the overall teaching of the Bible and it cannot contradict what the Bible clearly teaches elsewhere. The Bible cannot contradict itself. This is a true principle of Bible interpretation. All spiritual gifts should be exercised in faith, looking to God, looking to His Word, looking to maintain a healthy relationship with Christ.

St Paul lists seven kinds of gifts in Rom12:6-8: prophecy, service, teaching, exhortation, giving, leading, mercy. What's amazing about this list is that at least four of them are virtues that all Christians must have in order to be obedient Christians. These are:

Service: since St Paul calls all Christians to "serve one another in love," Gal 5:13.

Exhortation: since he commands all Christians to "exhort one another day after day," Heb3:13.

Giving: because St Paul calls all Christians to "share with him who has need," Eph4:28.

Mercy: because Our Lord Jesus says to all Christians, "Be merciful as your Father is merciful," Lk6:36.

The Spiritual Gift of Prophecy

The spiritual gift of prophecy is listed among the gifts of the Spirit in 1Co12:10 and Rom12:6. The Greek word translated "prophesying" or "prophecy" in both passages properly means to "speak forth" or declare the divine will, to interpret the purposes of God, or to make known in any way the truth of God which is designed to influence people. Many people misunderstand the gift of prophecy to be the ability to predict the future. While knowing something about the future may sometimes have been an aspect of the gift of prophecy, it was primarily a gift of proclamation ("forth-telling"), not prediction ("fore-telling"). It is more accurately "forth-telling" the heart and mind of God, which may or may not include a predictive aspect. A pastor/preacher who declares the Bible can be considered a "prophesier" in that he is speaking forth the counsel of God.

> Prophecy means primarily the explanation of things which are unclear, whether future or past, whether present or hidden.
>
> – St Diodore

The gift of prophet seems to have been a temporary gift given by Christ for the laying of the foundation of the Church. Prophets were foundational to the Church (Eph2:20). The prophet proclaimed a message from the Lord to the early believers. Sometimes a prophet's message was revelatory (new revelation and truth from God) and sometimes a prophet's message was predictive (Acts11:28 and 21:10). The early Christians did not have the complete Bible. Some early Christians did not have access to any of the books of the New Testament. The New Testament prophets "filled the gap" by proclaiming God's message to the people who would not have access to it otherwise. The last book of the New Testament (Revelation) was not completed until late in the first century. So, the Lord sent prophets to proclaim God's Word to His people.

With the completion of the New Testament canon, prophesying changed from declaring new revelation to declaring the completed revelation God has already given. Jude 3 speaks of "the faith which was once delivered unto the saints." In other words, the faith to which we hold has been settled forever, and it does not need the addition or refinement that comes from extra-biblical revelations.

Are there true prophets today? If the purpose of a prophet was to reveal truth from God, why would we need prophets if we have the completed revelation from God in the Bible? That the gift of prophecy was a temporary gift is strongly suggested by Eph2:20 (a foundation is only laid once). If prophets were the "foundation" of the early Church, are we still building the "foundation" today? Also, if prophesy were given today, then this would mean that the Bible is not complete and not sufficient for the Church. It would mean that we need additional revelation and that what we have in our Bible is not enough. God's Word is totally sufficient for the Church today. Can God give someone a message to deliver to someone else? Absolutely! Does God reveal truth to someone in a supernatural way and enable that person to deliver that message to others? Absolutely! But is this the biblical gift of prophecy? No.

Also, note the transition from prophet to teacher in 2Pt2:1: "There were false prophets among the people, even as there shall be false teachers among you." St Peter indicates that the Old Testament age had prophets, whereas the Church will have teachers. The spiritual gift of prophecy, in the sense of receiving new revelations from God to be proclaimed to others, ceased with the completion of the Bible. During the time that prophecy was a revelatory gift, it was to be used for the edification, exhortation, and comfort of men (1Co14:3). The modern gift of prophecy, which is really more related to teaching, still declares the truth of God. What has changed is that the truth of God today has already been fully revealed in His Word, while, in the early Church, it had not yet been fully revealed.

Christians are to be very wary of those who claim to have a "new" message from God. It is one thing to say, "I had an interesting dream last night." However, it is quite another matter to say, "God gave me a dream last night, and you must obey it." No utterance of man should be considered equal to or above the written Word. We must hold to the Word that God has already given and commit ourselves to sola scriptura — Scripture alone. "Do not despise prophecies, but test everything; hold fast what is good," 1Th5:20-21. In other words, it sounds as if some of what comes by way of prophecies is good — hold fast to that — and some is not — let that go. In other words, the gift of prophecy is not in the same category with Scripture. It is under Scripture and tested by Scripture, and it is spiritual wisdom informed by Scripture.

If your gift is prophesying, St Paul is cautioning that prophecy must be according to the faith, in accord with the accepted body of doctrine among believers. Those who prophesy should stick to the faith, not their own opinions, to strengthen, encourage, comfort and edify the Church (1Co14:3-4). The one who prophesies speaks to people for their up-building and encouragement and consolation. St Paul says to the Church in Corinth, "Pursue love, and earnestly desire the spiritual gifts, especially that you may prophesy,"1Co14:1. So all of us are told to earnestly desire especially to prophesy.

Then, using the gift in proportion to our faith will mean that we use it to exalt Christ. That's what faith does. Using the gift in proportion to our faith means that we will use it both humbly and boldly. Finally, using the gift in proportion to our faith means that we will make love the measure of what we say, because "faith works through love" (Gal 5:6). "If I speak in the tongues of men and of angels, but have not love, I am a noisy gong or a clanging cymbal. And if I have prophetic powers, and understand all mysteries and all knowledge, and if I have all faith, so as to remove mountains, but have not love, I am nothing," 1Co13:1-2. Therefore, "Use the gift of prophecy in proportion to your faith," Rom12:6 means, 'use it to love and build each other up in faith to the glory of Christ.'

The Spiritual Gift of Ministry

"Ministry" is from the Greek word 'diakoneo', meaning "to serve" or 'douleuo', meaning "to serve as a slave". 'Diakonos' is a noun meaning "a person who serves". We get the English word "deacon" from it. Diakoneo is the verb form of 'diakonos'; it means "serve". In the New Testament, ministry is seen as service to God and to other people in His name. Our Lord Jesus provided the pattern for Christian ministry: He came, not to receive service, but to give it (Mt20:28; Mk10:45; Jn13:1-17). The most specific meaning of 'diakoneo' is to work with food to serve other people. Martha "served" at a dinner (Jn12:2; Lk10:40). Our Lord Jesus told parables about servants who were expected to prepare food and serve their masters (Lk17:8; 22:27). In the early Church, seven men were chosen "to wait on tables" (Acts6:2-3).

'Diakoneo' can refer to more general types of service, too. Our Lord Jesus served His disciples (Mt20:28; Mk10:45). Jesus' disciples should also serve (Lk22:27; Jn12:26). When we serve others, we are showing love to God (Heb6:10) — a point also made in the parable of sheep and goats. This parable shows that serving can include not only supplying food and drink, but also clothing and other needs (Mt25:44). 'Diakonia' is often used to refer to a spiritual ministry. The apostles had a "ministry of the word" (Acts6:4). St Paul said that his ministry was "the task of testifying to the Gospel of God's Grace" (Acts20:24). St Paul's message of reconciliation was his ministry (2Co5:18). The new covenant is a "ministry that brings righteousness" (2Co3:8-9).

Everyone should serve (in a general sense), but each serves in a different way — some serve by speaking and some serve by manual labour. It is this latter type of service that forms the core of the office of deacon (1Ti3:10, 13). No matter what type of serving is done, it should be done with the strength God provides, so that He gets the praise and glory (1Pt4:11).

St Paul used the word 'diakonos' to describe himself as a servant of the Lord (1Co3:5), a servant of God (2Co6:4), a servant of the new covenant (2Co3:6), a servant of the Gospel (Eph3:7; Col 1:23) and a servant of the church (Col 1:2325). Also, he frequently called himself a 'doulos' — a slave or servant of Our Lord Jesus Christ. In Jewish society, a 'doulos' was usually a servant. In Greek society, he was usually a slave. However, this type of service is not restricted to slaves and apostles — it is commanded for all Christians. This is another description of our ministry. Christ himself took on the nature of a servant (Php2:7), and He quoted the proverb, "No servant is greater than his master," Mt10:24-25; Jn15:20-21. Since our Master served as a servant, shouldn't we also be servants? In Christianity, greatness is measured by service. "Whoever wants to be first must be slave of all," Mt20:27; Mk10:44.

'Doulos' also has metaphorical uses — sinners are slaves of whatever has power over them (2Pt2:19). Christ frees us from the slavery of the fear of death (Heb2:15). He frees us from the slavery of sin (Jn8:34; Rom6:16-20) by redeeming us, purchasing us with His own blood. He frees us from "the yoke of slavery" (Gal 5:1) so that we may serve Him in the new way of the Spirit (Rom7:6). We become slaves to obedience, slaves to righteousness (Rom6:16-22). Christians are "slaves of Christ" (1Co7:22; Eph6:6).

We are all admonished to serve the Lord (Rom12:11; 14:18; 1Th1:9), and one of the primary responsibilities our Lord and Master gives us is to serve one another in love (Gal 5:13). As slaves of Christ and slaves of one another, we serve one another by using the gifts God gives us. Those who have been given a gift of (manual) ministry should use that gift (Rom12:7). Those who have other gifts should likewise use them to serve others (1Pt4:10).

In Php1:1 and 1Ti3:8-13 it denotes an office in the Church. But almost everywhere else, the word is used in a more general sense. It refers to apostles, preachers and lay members more often than it does to deacons. The general sense of the word is "assistant". It indicates not just work in general, but work that benefits someone else. The content of ministry seems to prioritize the ministering in spiritual things, not just practical things. Ministry should certainly place emphasis on sharing the Gospel of Our Lord Jesus Christ with others so they can come to know Him and receive Him as personal Saviour, go on to experience Him as Lord of their life, and go even further to know Christ as the essence of their Life (Jn1:12; Col 2:6-7; Gal 2:20; Php3:8-10). The ministry in our day has taken on more of a vocational meaning as we call pastors "ministers" to full-time service. Pastors do spend their lives in the ministry, they do minister to others, and they can rightly be designated as ministers.

> The word 'service' or 'ministry' is comprehensive, covering everything from the apostleship itself to any spiritual function.
>
> — John Chrysostom

But pastors are not the only ones who are to be involved in ministry. All Christians—whether men, women, deacons or priests (elders) — are called to be ministers. From the early New Testament churches to the churches of our day, each Christian should be in the ministry of helping others (Rom12:3-8, 10-13; 2Ti2:24-26). Christians are commanded to serve one another. None of the words for service or ministry is restricted to the ordained clergy. All members are enslaved to one another. We all have obligations to one another. Whether our service is in word or in deed, it is a religious duty for all Christians. Whether we are ordained or not, we are all called to serve the Lord by serving one another.

As slave-servants, we are ministering to one another, to the church, to the Gospel and to the Lord. God has given each of us a ministry. We should minister to one another's needs. God has given us abilities so that we will use them to serve others. The Christian should minister by meeting people's needs with love and humility on Christ's behalf (Mt20:26; Mk10:43; Jn2:5,9; Acts6:3; Rom1:1; Gal 1:10; Col 4:12). Christians are to minister to others out of their devotion to Christ and their love for others, whether the other people are believers or unbelievers. Ministry to others should be impartial and unconditional, always seeking to help others as Our Lord Jesus would. Ministry can, and should, include ministering to the physical, emotional, mental, vocational, and financial needs of others. Our Lord Jesus did, and so should we!

The Spiritual Gift of Teaching

The spiritual gift of teaching is one of the gifts of the Holy Spirit (Rom12:6-8; 1Co12:28; Eph4:1-12). It is a gift given by the Holy Spirit, enabling one to effectively communicate the truths of the Bible to others. It is most often, but not always, used in the context of the local church. The gift of teaching involves the analysis and proclamation of the Word of God, explaining the meaning, context, and application to the hearer's life. The gifted teacher is one who has the unique ability to clearly instruct and communicate knowledge, specifically the doctrines of the faith and truths of the Bible. The teacher is to saturate people with doctrine and with truth.

The Greek word for "teach" is 'didaskalos', which means "to instruct". We see examples all through the Bible of teaching. Our Lord Jesus Himself was the Great Teacher, and Our Lord Jesus commanded His disciples to "go and make disciples of all nations, baptizing them in the name of the Father and of the Son and of the Holy Spirit, and teaching them to obey everything I have commanded you," Mt28:19–20. Our Lord Jesus commanded His disciples to teach new disciples everything He had commanded, instructing them in both doctrine and holy living. Christ's ministers are not to teach the commandments of men or anything that is of their own or other men's devising, but only that which is ordered by Christ.

'Teaching' means instruction in the commands of God.

— St Theodoret

There are several contexts in which the gift of teaching can be used: Sunday school classes, Bible schools, colleges, seminaries, and home Bible studies. The one with the gift can teach either individuals or groups. A person with the natural talent to teach can teach just about anything, but a person with the spiritual gift of teaching teaches the content of the Bible. He can teach the message of a book as a whole book or break it down to individual paragraphs or verses. No new material originates from one with the gift of teaching. The teacher simply explains or expounds the meaning of the Bible's text.

Teaching is a supernatural gift of the Holy Spirit. One without this gift can understand the Bible as he hears or reads it, but he cannot explain it as one with the gift can. All believers ought to be able to teach and share truth to some degree, but some believers are especially gifted at this. Although it can be developed, the spiritual gift of teaching is not something that can be learned or acquired, as with a college degree. A person with a PhD but without the gift of teaching will not be able to expound the Bible as one without a degree but having the gift of teaching.

In Eph4:11, teachers are linked with pastors. This does not necessarily suggest one gift, but it does seem to imply that the pastor is also a teacher. The Greek word for pastor is 'poiemen' which means 'shepherd'. A pastor is one who cares for his people in the same way a shepherd cares for his sheep. Just as a shepherd feeds his sheep, the pastor also has the responsibility to teach his people the spiritual food of the Word of God. The church is edified through use of the gift of teaching as people listen to the Word of God and hear what it means and how to apply it to their own lives. God has raised up many with this gift to build people up in their faith and enable them to grow in all wisdom and knowledge (2Pt3:18).

A difference between a teacher and prophet is this: A prophet gets his message directly from God with the result that what he says is inspired speech: "Thus says the Lord!" A teacher gets his message by diligently studying the Word of God in prayerful dependence upon the illuminating ministry of the Holy Spirit. The prophet gives forth the Word of God. The teacher explains and proclaims God's Word (but not under direct inspiration). The teacher's explanations of God's Word may be fallible. He needs to lean hard upon the Lord for understanding, praying that the Lord will guide him to the true interpretation of Scripture and keep him from error.

How can Christians know if they have the gift of teaching? They should begin by asking God for opportunities to teach a Sunday school class or Bible study, under the authority and guidance of a gifted teacher. If they find they can explain the meaning of the Bible and others respond favourably, they probably have the gift and should ask God for further opportunities to use and develop their gift.

The Spiritual Gift of Exhortation

The gift of exhortation is often called the gift of encouragement. God's people need words of comfort and encouragement. The primary means of exhortation is to remind the hearer of the powerful and amazing work of God in Christ, particularly in regard to the saving work of Our Lord Jesus in the atonement. We see St Paul commanding St Titus to use this gift in Tts1:9 and throughout chapter 2, particularly Tts2:11-15. He also charges St Timothy in 2Ti4:2.

The Spirit of God gives this gift to people in the church to strengthen and encourage those who are wavering in their faith. Those with the gift of exhortation can uplift and motivate others as well as challenge and rebuke them in order to foster spiritual growth and action. The goal of the encourager is to see everyone in the church continually building up the body of Christ and glorifying God. People with this gift are often involved in teaching, counselling, and discipleship training ministries within the church. Exhorters are among the first to find believers who are floundering in their faith. They come alongside the weaker ones to encourage, confront, if necessary, and model victorious living.

People with the gift of exhortation do not merely proclaim truth, as prophets often do. They develop relationships, often taking time to do those little extras that make the difference when someone is struggling. Rather than say, "You should begin reading the Psalms every day", an exhorter might say, "Let's start a Bible study together on Psalms. How about coffee Tuesday morning?" We are instructed to earnestly desire spiritual gifts, which implies that, as we are faithful with the ones we have been given, God will entrust us with more (1Co12:31; 14:1). Regardless of our primary gifts, all Christians should desire to become better at exhortation to build up those who are weaker, encourage those who lead, and strengthen the Body of Christ (1Th5:14; 2Co1:4). We all should do this (Heb3:13; 10:25) but some are especially gifted at this. We don't want to be "miserable comforters" like the friends of Job!

For the next three gifts, St Paul adds an adverb to emphasize the way we should serve: "If it is giving, then give generously; if it is to lead, do it diligently; if it is to show mercy, do it cheerfully," Rom12:8.

The Spiritual Gift of Giving

Christ gave Himself as a ransom for our sins. And so one of the gifts of the Spirit is the gift of giving. So St Paul tells us that he that gives, let him do it with simplicity. Now the Bible tells us several things concerning our giving, as far as how we are to give. First of all, we are to give willingly from our hearts. When the children of Israel were going to make the tabernacle, God gave to Moses the design of the various instruments that were to be used. It was to be made of silver and gold that was to cover the ark of the covenant and the cherubim. And it was going to take a lot of silver, a lot of gold, and a lot of special types of cloth. And so, the Lord spoke unto Moses, "Speak unto the children of Israel, that they bring me an offering: of every man that gives it willingly with his heart you shall take my offering," Ex25:2.

Now God did not want anybody to give who was not giving willingly or giving from their heart. God never wants a person to feel pressured in giving to Him. Whatever you give to God, you should always give willingly and from your heart. And you should only give that which you can give willingly from your heart. Now from a negative side concerning our giving, it should never be done out of pressure or grudgingly. "According as he has purposed in his heart, so let him give," 2Co9:7. We are not to give out of constraint, but just as we have purposed in our own hearts.

The blessing comes from cheerful giving. It comes when I give willingly from my heart; and then I am blessed. I give out of love for the Lord and because I love Him, I want to do something special. I am often feeling like, "Oh, Lord, You have done so much. I just want to do something special and make a sacrifice." And I am just loving Him as

I do it. Then God blesses that and God honours that.

Surely Our Lord Jesus indicated that it is not the amount that is given (Mark 12) as He was watching with His disciples and the people were putting their money in the treasury offering. And the wealthy were coming with all their pomp and circumstance and glory, putting in their large gifts. Then one little widow came up and dropped in a quarter of a cent. And Our Lord Jesus turned to His disciples, and said, "Did you see that? She gave more than all the rest-because they just gave from their surplus. This woman gave her very livelihood. That is all she had." In the Lord's eyes it is not the amount that is given, it is the heart that is behind the giving and what it has cost you to give.

Interestingly, the Lord loves sacrificial giving and this is something that seems quite rare. But if a person has the gift of giving, they really do not think of it as a sacrifice. They think, "Oh, praise the Lord! I am glad I can give."

The Spiritual Gift of Leadership

There are several characteristics of those with the spiritual gift of leadership. First and foremost, they recognize that their position is by the appointment of the Lord and is under His direction. They understand that they are not absolute rulers but are themselves subject to the One who is over them all, the Lord Jesus who is the Head of the Church. Recognizing his place in the hierarchy of the administration of the body of Christ prevents the gifted leader from succumbing to pride or a sense of entitlement. The truly gifted Christian leader recognizes that he is but a slave of Christ and a servant of those he leads. The apostle St Paul recognized this position, referring to himself as a "servant of Christ Jesus" (Rom1:1). Like St Paul, the gifted leader recognizes that God has called him to his position; he has not called himself (1Co1:1). Following Jesus' example, the gifted leader also lives to serve those he leads, and not to be served by them or lord it over them (Mt20:25-28).

The apostle James, the cousin of the Lord Jesus, had the gift of leadership as he led the Church in Jerusalem. He, too, referred to himself as "a servant of God and of the Lord Jesus Christ" (Jam1:1). St James exhibited another quality of spiritual leadership — the ability to sway others to think rightly, biblically, and godly in all matters. At the Jerusalem Council, St James dealt with the contentious issue of how to relate to Gentiles coming to faith in Our Lord Jesus the Messiah. "And after they had become silent, James answered, saying, 'Men and brethren, listen to me: Simon has declared how God at the first visited the Gentiles to take out of them a people for His Name'," Acts15:13-14. With that opening statement, James led the delegates to think clearly and biblically, enabling them to come to a right decision on this issue (Acts15:22-29).

As shepherds of God's people, gifted leaders rule with diligence and possess the ability to discern true spiritual needs from "felt" needs. They lead others to maturity in the faith. The Christian leader leads others to grow in their ability to discern for themselves that which comes from God versus that which is cultural or temporary. Following St Paul's example, the Church leader's words are not "wise and persuasive" from the viewpoint of human wisdom but are filled with the power of the Holy Spirit, leading and encouraging others to rest their faith on that very power (1Co2:4-6). The goal of the gifted leader is to guard and guide those he leads "until we all attain to the unity of the faith and of the knowledge of the Son of God, to mature manhood, to the measure of the stature of the fullness of Christ," Eph4:13. The spiritual gift of leadership is given by God to men and women who will help the Church to grow and thrive beyond the current generation. God has given the gift of leadership not to exalt men but to glorify Himself when believers use His gifts to do His will.

The Spiritual Gift of Mercy

"Blessed are the merciful: for they shall obtain mercy," Mt5:7. Mercy is what we express when we are led by God to be compassionate in our attitudes, words, and actions. It is more than feeling sympathy toward someone; it is love enacted. Mercy desires to answer the immediate needs of others and alleviate suffering, loneliness, and grief. Mercy addresses physical, emotional, financial, or spiritual crises with generous, self-sacrificial service. Mercy is a champion of the lowly, poor, exploited, and forgotten and often acts on their behalf.

This gift has a practical application of active service as well as a responsibility to do so cheerfully (Rom12:8). Additionally, we are all called to be merciful. Our Lord Jesus says that "whatever you did for one of the least of these brothers and sisters of mine, you did for Me," Mt25:40.

Mercy is promised to those who are merciful toward others (Mt5:7). As spiritually dead and blind sinners, we are no better off than the two blind men in Matthew 20. Just as they were utterly dependent on Christ's compassion to restore their sight, so are we dependent on Him to "show us His mercy and grant us His salvation" (Ps85:7). This bedrock understanding that our hope depends on Christ's mercy alone and not in any merit of ours should inspire us to follow Christ's example of compassionate service and show mercy to others as it has been shown to us.

How to Use Our Gifts Matters

All service should be sincere; gifts should be motivated by generosity; mercy should be given joyfully. What matters to God is not merely that we use our gifts, but how we use them — the spirit, the attitude. What matters is not merely that we give and lead and show mercy. What matters to God, is free and lavish generosity in our giving. What matters to God, is passion and eagerness and zeal in our leadership. What matters to God, is gladness and cheerfulness and joy in our mercy. Humility is not mainly self-condemnation (there is plenty to condemn in ourselves, and if we think about it we should do it), but little ministry is produced with that kind of self-focus.

What unleashes ministry is the positive side of humility: the overflow of humble joy in the mercy of Christ.

St Paul does not give these commands as requirements for salvation. Rather, these are what we should do after being saved, after God has shown us His mercy. When you don't think too highly of yourself, but you forget about yourself and are filled with love to Christ, your ministry has the character of overflow. In giving, your joy in Christ overflows with generosity. In leading, your joy in Christ overflows with zeal. In mercy, your joy in Christ overflows with cheerfulness. These three words (generosity, zeal, joy) are meant to show us that Christian ministry is not duty-driven or begrudging. It's the overflow of a self-forgetting, happy relationship with Christ.

In giving St Paul looks for liberality; in showing mercy for cheerfulness; in care giving for diligence. For it is not with money that St Paul wants us to help those in need but with words, deeds, in person or in every other way.

— John Chrysostom

It is of vital importance to recognize that the Scriptures emphasize the greatest gift of all: the gift of God's life which is the present possession of every believer (1Jn5:11-12; Rom6:23; Jn6:47). No believer is without this gift! It is our responsibility first and foremost to seek to manifest the resurrected life of our Lord Jesus Christ (2Co4:10-11; Gal 2:20; 4:19; 5:22-23) by the power of the indwelling Holy Spirit. Each member of the body of Christ needs to be staying in a healthy and right relationship with the Lord Jesus Christ, abiding in Him as the True Vine (Jn15:1-5). He is our Life! (Col 3:4) As we stay in a healthy relationship with Christ, God will develop our gift or gifts for His glory and for the benefit of the local assembly of which we are a part.

Thus St Paul in Rom12:6-8 mentions seven distinct and different gifts. This is just a sample list of gifts, certainly not exhaustive. One of these gifts, prophecy, was a temporary gift which has since been "done away" (1Co13:8) but the others are gifts still needed in the local churches today.

It is of vital importance to recognize that the Scriptures emphasize the greatest gift of all: the gift of God's life which is the present possession of every believer (1Jn5:11-

12; Rom6:23; Jn6:47). No believer is without this gift! It is our responsibility first and foremost to seek to manifest the resurrected life of our Lord Jesus Christ (2Co4:10-11; Gal 2:20; 4:19; 5:22-23) by the power of the indwelling Holy Spirit. Each member of the body of Christ needs to be staying in a healthy and right relationship with the Lord Jesus Christ, abiding in Him as the True Vine (Jn15:1-5). He is our Life! (Col 3:4) As we stay in a healthy relationship with Christ, God will develop our gift or gifts for His glory and for the benefit of the local assembly of which we are a part.

HARMONY IN THE
BODY OF CHRIST

"Let love be without hypocrisy. Abhor what is evil. Cling to what is good. Be kindly affectionate to one another with brotherly love, in honour giving preference to one another; not lagging in diligence, fervent in spirit, serving the Lord; rejoicing in hope, patient in tribulation, continuing steadfastly in prayer; distributing to the needs of the saints, given to hospitality," Rom 12:9-13

In Rom12:9-13, St Paul is focusing on attitudes within the Christian community. The five verses contain 13 exhortations so that we can live in harmony with each other. This section shows one thing clearly: St Paul knew the teaching of Jesus, especially the Sermon on the Mount. St Paul begins to list some qualities that should characterize Christian love. He begins with a general principle: "Let love be without hypocrisy. Abhor that which is evil. Cling to what is good," Rom 12:9.

Abhor What Is Evil; Cling to What Is Good

So how can we live out true love? In Rom12:9b, St Paul defines true love with two participles that function like commands: "Abhor what is evil; cling to what is good." Although this verse is a broad Christian principle, St Paul seems to apply it to all that follows in Rom12:10-21. The word translated "abhor" is only used here in the entire New Testament. It means "to have a vehement dislike for something, hate strongly". True love does not tolerate evil. In the same breath, St Paul says you are to also "cling to what is good." The verb "cling" can mean "to glue". St Paul wants us to be intimately glued to that which is good. Christians ought to be known for their love (Jn13:35) and they also should be known for their hate. We must hate the things which our God hates, and be attached and devoted to that which is good.

Nobody doubts that the soul has feelings of hatred in it; however, it is praiseworthy to hate evil and to hate sin. For unless a person hates evil he cannot love, nor can he retain the virtues. For example, if someone intends to preserve chastity, he cannot keep it safe unless he hates and despise immodesty.

– Origen

Love Without Hypocrisy

Love is not a vague feeling, but it discerns the difference between good and bad. In some way, it is often easier for us to either abhor what is evil or cling to what is good rather than doing both; the godly person knows how to practice both. Love without action is not love. Love should be without hypocrisy. Of course, love with hypocrisy isn't real love at all; but much of what masquerades as "love" in the Christian community is laced with hypocrisy, and must be demonstrated against.

What is hypocrisy? Hypocrisy shows itself in two ways. One is that it tries to make the outside look better than the inside. We put forward what looks like a loving behaviour that does not really signify what we feel inside — just as St Paul said, "If I give away all I have, and if I deliver up my body to be burned, but have not love, I gain nothing," 1Co13:3. So you can do some remarkable external acts of sacrifice and not have love. The classic statement of this form of hypocrisy is what Our Lord Jesus said, "You hypocrites! Well did Isaiah prophesy of you, when he said: 'This people honours me with their lips, but their heart is far from me'," Mt15:7. External lip-praise was not accompanied by internal heart-praise. Our Lord Jesus called this hypocrisy.

Few things brought down His wrath like hypocrisy. Hypocrisy is driven by the craving for other people to make much of us. For example, Our Lord Jesus said, "When you give to the needy, sound no trumpet before you, as the hypocrites do in the synagogues and in the streets, that they may be praised by others. Truly, I say to you, they have received their reward," Mt6:2. "And when you pray, you must not be like the hypocrites. For they love to stand and pray in the synagogues and at the street corners, that they may be seen by others. Truly, I say to you, they have received their reward," Mt6:5.

Love is not like that, St Paul says. It is not hypocritical. It does not crave the praise of men. It has been set free from that bondage. In fact, that is close to the essence of love: It doesn't think highly of itself — it doesn't think much about itself at all. It is riveted on Christ and all that God is for us in Him. The command to love without hypocrisy is really a command to know Christ and love Christ and find your satisfaction in Christ so that you do not crave the praise of men any more.

First, there is the aim to get and keep the praise and

approval of other people. But there is another evil that hypocrisy sometimes aims at. Most commonly we think of hypocrisy aiming at the praise of others. So there is a kind of posturing and posing. But there is a more subtle aim for hypocrisy, namely, to cover sins that may have nothing to do with how we are posturing and posing. It shows itself when we hide internal sin by putting up a moral, external front. For example, Our Lord Jesus said, "Woe to you, scribes and Pharisees, hypocrites! For you clean the outside of the cup and the plate, but inside they are full of greed and self-indulgence. . .. Woe to you, scribes and Pharisees, hypocrites! For you are like whitewashed tombs, which outwardly appear beautiful, but within are full of dead people's bones and all uncleanness," Mt23:25, 27.

For example, in Luke 13 Our Lord Jesus heals a woman who had been bent over for 18 years. It was the Sabbath. So the ruler of the synagogue was angry and said, "There are six days in which work ought to be done. Come on those days and be healed, and not on the Sabbath day." Then the Lord Our Lord Jesus answered him, "You hypocrites!

Does not each of you on the Sabbath untie his ox or his donkey from the manger and lead it away to water it?" Lk13:14-15.

Our Lord Jesus called this man's zeal for the Sabbath hypocrisy. Why? It wasn't so much that he was seeking the praise of men. He was a hypocrite because his religious zeal was hiding something. What was this man concealing? "Does not each of you on the Sabbath untie his ox or his donkey and lead it away to water it?" Bottom line: money! (Lk16:14.) You don't give a rip about this woman! But you care about your ox and your donkey! Your zeal for the Lord's day is sheer hypocrisy.

We hide our own flaws (sometimes even from ourselves) by drawing attention to other people's flaws so that ours don't show up so clearly. This I would suggest is found most frequently in marriage troubles. But not only there. For example, Our Lord Jesus said, "How can you say to your brother, 'Brother, let me take out the speck that is in your eye,' when you yourself do not see the log that is in your own eye? You hypocrite, first take the log out of your own eye, and then you will see clearly to take out the speck that is in your brother's eye," Lk6:42.

St Paul is saying: real love doesn't act this way. Let love be without hypocrisy. It isn't love if it is hypocrisy. He said in 1Co13:6 that love "rejoices with the truth." But hypocrisy is all about falsehood, concealment, deceit, cloaking, misleading, hiding. Hypocrisy is the opposite of loving the truth. So it is the opposite of love. So, St Paul says, let love be without hypocrisy. Let it be genuine.

Love doesn't put up artificial fronts. Love does not dwell on the flaws of others. Love does not crave the praise of men. And love does not act religious to hide sin. Love forgets itself and looks to Christ and overflows with joy in Him to meet the needs of others. So let us look to Christ for everything we need.

Brotherly Affection

"Be kindly affectionate to one another with brotherly love in honour giving preference to one another," Rom12:10. "Love" and "brotherly affection," are emotion-laden words. "Brotherly affection" is just what it says. It's the affection of a family that comes with long familiarity and deep bonds. Of course you can have squabbles and get mad, but let some bully pick on your brother, and the family affection shows a powerful side. Or let one of the family members get a life-threatening sickness or even die, and there will be a kind of tears that do not come for others. This is what we are supposed to have for each other in the church.

Be kindly affectionate to one another is appropriate for the "family" of Christ; a cold, stand-offish attitude has no place among Christians. "Preferring one another": in humble-mindedness I should consider my fellow believer to be better than myself (Php2:3). How blinded by pride is the person who always sees himself as better and superior to others.

Give Honour

Honour is different from affection. You can honour a person for whom you have no affection. St Paul doesn't want you to choose between these. Do both he says. But they are different. Honouring someone is treating them with your deeds and your words as worthy of your service. They may not be worthy of it. But you can do it anyway. Some honouring means treating people better than they deserve. Prefer to honour rather than be honoured. If you try to out-honour someone it means you love to honour more than you love to be honoured. You enjoy elevating others to honour more than you enjoy being elevated to honour. So don't be giving energy to how you can be honoured, but how you can honour. Put to death the craving for honour. Cultivate the love of honouring others.

In honour giving preference to one another is a way that shows that the displays of affection are genuine. Affection for God brings affection for His children. We will spend eternity with each other in the sweetest possible relationships. There will be no suspicion or animosity or resentment or disapproval in heaven. God commands us to live in the light of that family reality now. And the preference to honour others more than to be honoured is also a natural fruit and demonstration that we have been so incredibly honoured by God and that nature is in us. We are not honourable in relation to God. We are infinitely dishonourable to God in ourselves.

We have brought great discredit on God for how little we love Him and how much we prefer other things to Him. Nevertheless, God has given His Son on our behalf while we were yet sinners (Rom5:6) — while we were yet dishonouring Him — and honoured us by rescuing us from sin and death and hell and Satan and by giving us a place at His table. And beyond all natural comprehension the sovereign Son of God not only honoured us by washing our feet while He was here on earth (Jn13:1), but in Lk12:37 it pictures the second coming like this: "He will dress himself for service and have them recline at table, and he will come and serve them."

Most people struggle to get more honour, but as we imitate our Saviour, we should try to excel in humility and give more honour. Our status is secure in Christ, so we do not need to fight for it. We have been so immeasurably honoured in mercy that not to prefer to honour as we have been honoured is to betray that we have not tasted the treasure of our salvation. Loving with affection and preferring to honour are important because they show our new nature in Christ. That is the way children of God treat each other. It's in their spiritual DNA.

behaviours that are natural and fitting for those who are regenerated in Baptism and are indwelt by the Holy Spirit and are justified by faith and are treasuring Christ and are hoping in the glory of God. These are behaviours that are fitting and natural and proper. They come like fruit.

Second, God demands that we love with affection and prefer to honour each other because this strengthens and confirms the faith of those we love affectionately and honour. When you are on the receiving end of affection and merciful honour in the body of Christ you experience the confirmation that you are indeed in the family. God means for all things to be done for the up building of that confidence and joy (1Co14:26). Loving with affection and preferring to honour are two ways of confirming and strengthening the faith of others.

Third, God demands that we love with affection and prefer to honour over being honoured because this displays the glory of Christ, because He is the one who enables us to live this way and this is a portrait of His own character. Eph4:32 says, "Be kind to one another, tender-hearted, forgiving one another, as God in Christ forgave you." The tenderness of our relations is rooted in the tenderness of God in Christ. And when we elevate someone by becoming their servant, we are painting a picture of the way Christ was among us. So loving affectionately and preferring to honour displays the glory of Christ.

Fourth, God demands that we love with affection and honour each other because this lures the world to love Him and all that He is for them in Christ. When you magnify Christ by loving Christians affectionately and outdoing each other in showing honour, the world will see and be more inclined to glorify God (Mt5:16). In other words, there are reasons for why St Paul commands us to love each other with affection and outdo one another in showing honour. These things are like branches, or fruit, on the tree of faith. They belong to the very nature of who we are in Christ.

Finally, how do you have affection for a believer you may not even like? How do you honour a believer who may do dishonourable things? Everything in the Bible is written to answer this question. Because everything God does, He does to make His children what we ought to be. So receive everything from God as a means of grace to make you love with affection and honour others.

Consider the analogy in marriage. Do you think that

married couples always feel tender affection for each other? Always feel tender and warm? They don't. But such affection is the ideal. That is what God calls us to. Be devoted to one another in love. Honour one another above yourselves. And one of the reasons He makes marriage unbreakable and seals it with an oath, "For better or for worse, till death do us part," is because He knows that we need to live our lives in the circle of rugged commitment where feelings of absolute hopelessness that affection could ever be awakened again can indeed be overcome and true, new tender affections revived. I know that it can happen. It has happened.

That is not only true in marriage. It is true in the church. Remember how this chapter begins: "I appeal to you therefore, brothers, by the mercies of God," Rom12:1. Yes, by the mercies of God, we will love each other with brotherly affection. By the mercies of God, we will outdo one another in showing honour.

SERVING THE LORD

"Not lagging in diligence, fervent in spirit, serving the Lord," Rom12:11. All of life is a serving of the Lord. We do not serve the Lord one day a week and serve some other god on the other six. This is a verse about life. About living life as to the Lord, whether we are eating or drinking or whatever we are doing — to do it in the name of the Lord and for the glory of the Lord, since all of life belongs to the Lord. That includes all your family life and vocational life and leisure life and civic life and political life. So this verse is about how we deal with significant issues in public life.

With Zeal

St Paul is saying: 'when it comes to serving Christ, half-heartedness, luke-warmness, laziness, sluggishness, slothfulness is utterly inappropriate.' Being saved by Our Lord Jesus Christ is the greatest thing in the world. It means having eternal life. You cannot die. You will live forever in overwhelming joy. Nothing can separate you from Christ. Everything works for your good. All your troubles and sorrows produce an eternal weight of glory. Not to be passionate about this is a sign of serious blindness or emotional disability.

Serving Christ is the highest privilege in the universe

for human beings. There are two phrases that describe how we are to serve the Lord. First we are to serve the Lord by "not lagging behind in diligence". Literally, "not lazy in earnestness". The RSV says, "Never flag in zeal". The NIV says, "Never be lacking in zeal". This is a rebuke to passivity and laziness and lethargy and apathy and boredom. St Paul assumes that if you see this in yourself you can do something about it. We have been given the Holy Spirit and the Word of God and the power of prayer precisely to fight against the encroachments of the passivity in our own hearts. Stir up zeal for God and for the cause of God and truth and life.

We are to be constantly serving the Lord as His love-slave. He is our blessed Master. God does not want lazy servants. He wants believers who are diligent and fervent

Fervently

Second, in verse 11, St Paul says, "(Be) fervent in spirit." The Greek word behind "fervent" is "zeontes" which means "boiling". That's where we get the English word "fervent", because it comes from the Latin word "to boil". Here is the positive side. Don't lag behind in diligence and earnestness and zeal, but rather, positively, "be fervent", "boil" in the spirit. Today we might say, "Be passionate" in your spirit. We exist to spread a passion for the supremacy of God in all things. The word "passion" is based squarely on Rom12:11, "boil in the spirit". "Be fervent in the spirit." "Boil in the Spirit."

"Never be lacking in zeal, but keep your spiritual fervour, serving the Lord," Rom12:11. Or as St Paul says in Gal 6:10, "Do not grow weary in doing good." It's not always easy or fun; we have to remember that we are serving God.

How is your spiritual temperature? Are you running a fever? Are you fervent? When it comes to enthusiasm for godly things, are you at the boiling point? In Acts 18:25 we learn of such a man!

> Daily meditation removes laziness and makes people vigilant.
>
> — St Ambrosiaster

Serve Our Lord Jesus not the Belly

First, St Paul says, serve Our Lord Jesus not the belly. "I appeal to you, brothers, to watch out for those who cause divisions and create obstacles contrary to the doctrine that you have been taught; avoid them. For such persons do not serve our Lord Christ, but their own appetites," Rom16:17-18. Literally, they serve their own belly.

So serving Christ is contrasted with serving your belly, which is shorthand for serving your appetites. You serve your appetites when you treat them as the most compelling offer of pleasure. If Christ calls you to self-control and chastity and purity of mind, and your appetites call you to self-indulgence and sexual license and impure thoughts, and you follow your appetites instead of Christ, you are serving them and not serving Christ. You are saying that they are a more compelling offer of pleasure. Serving

Christ does not measure up to what these appetites offer. That is a very serious thing to say.

This contrast between serving our appetites and serving the Lord draws our attention to the fact that serving Christ is better than eating food and serving Christ is better than sex (sexual intercourse, or pornography, or sexual fantasies, or masturbation), and serving Christ is better than the pleasures of laziness. So one thing we can say about serving Christ is that it means experiencing His worth and beauty and fellowship as more compelling and more desirable than what the appetites offer.

Serve Our Lord Jesus not People

Second, St Paul says, serve Our Lord Jesus not people. Now, of course, there is a sense in which we should serve people. He says, "Do not use your freedom as an opportunity for the flesh, but through love serve one another," Gal 5:13. We are to serve each other in the sense of doing good to each other, and meeting each other's' needs.

But there is another way that we serve people sometimes which is dead wrong. The wrong way to serve man is to be the slave to his approval. This is a great evil and a great bondage for many people. Many are servants of the opinions of others. Many people live with an eye to what others are thinking of them. Their happiness rises and falls with what other think and say.

St Paul says that the way to avoid this kind of service is to serve Christ instead. St Paul tells servants to work "not by the way of eye-service, as people-pleasers, but as servants of Christ, doing the will of God from the heart, rendering service with a good will as to the Lord and not to man," Eph6:6-7. That kind of service belongs ultimately to one person: Our Lord Jesus Christ. One audience matters ultimately. So the service of Our Lord Jesus in this sense is a great liberty. We are freed from the fickle opinions of men. We care for one thing: Does the Our Lord Jesus Christ, the Lord of heaven and earth, approve of what I am saying and doing?

This contrast between serving man and serving the Lord draws our attention to the fact that serving Christ is better than the approval of men. Pleasing Christ is infinitely more important than pleasing people. In fact, serving Christ can be defined as seeing Christ's approval as more valuable than the approval of man, and then acting on that conviction.

Serve Our Lord Jesus not the Law

Third, St Paul says, serve Our Lord Jesus not the Law. "But now we are released from the Law, having died to that which held us captive, so that we serve not under the old written code but in the new life of the Spirit," Rom7:6. St Paul contrasts serving under the old written code with serving in the new life of the Spirit. Once we focused on the demands of the Law for justification, and our service was deadly. No one is justified by works of the Law (Rom3:20). But now that Christ has come we have died to this focus on the Law and its demands and we focus on Christ and His Life-giving Spirit (Rom7:4).

What this means is that serving Christ is not mainly following a new Law. Rather now a Person, Our Lord Jesus Christ, stands where once the Law stood. And that divine Person is first and foremost a Law-fulfiller not a law demander. And in that way He is utterly unlike Moses. "It is fitting for us," Our Lord Jesus said, "to fulfil all righteousness" (Mt3:15). Christ redeemed us from the curse of the Law, by becoming a curse for us (Gal 3:13). He fulfils the Law perfectly and bears its curse perfectly.

Therefore, serving this Christ is radically different from serving Law. Serving a demand and serving a Divine Person who meets the demand before He makes the demand is radically different.

So serving Christ, not the Law, means believing who He is, the Messiah and Son of God, and believing what He has done, provided my perfect pardon and perfect righteousness, and then seeking with all our might to become in practice what we are in Him. This service is a great liberty. This slavery to Christ our righteousness is freedom and joy.

So we have seen that serving the Lord means:

• seeing the Lord as worth more than what the appetites offer;

• seeing the Lord's approval as more valuable than the approval of man and acting on it; and

• believing that He has died for us and fulfilled the Law for us so that all our serving is now receiving as a gift what He accomplished and what He bought.

In these three ways, St Paul shows us how we work with zeal and intensity and passion in the service of Christ, but that in all our working — all our serving — Christ is really giving to us what He bought and is the one serving us. For example, St Paul says "I will not venture to speak of anything except what Christ has accomplished through me to bring the Gentiles to obedience — by word and deed," Rom15:18. St Paul has served. Indeed, he has served with all his might and suffered greatly. But, he says, Christ has accomplished it all by working through me. My serving has been a receiving of Christ's serving me. My life is one constant trusting, and depending, and receiving.

All this emphasises that serving Christ is the greatest privilege in the world. It's true because the greatest Person in the universe has not just called us into His service, but has become our Servant so that all our serving is trusting and depending and receiving. And the reason He has done this is that the giver gets the glory. If we served Him because He needed something from us, we would get the glory. But if, as 1Pt4:11 says, we serve Him "in the strength that He supplies", then He gets the glory. In our serving Christ, we get the help, He gets the glory. This is the greatest life. Therefore, do not be slothful in zeal, but boil in the spirit as you serve the Lord.

CHRISTIAN ATTITUDE
IN TRIBULATION

"Rejoicing in hope; patient in tribulation; continuing steadfastly in prayer; distributing to the needs of the saints, given to hospitality," Rom12:12-13. Now, St Paul offers five exhortations dealing with your attitude towards difficult circumstances. Patience denotes not a passive putting up with things, but an active, steadfast endurance. Tribulation denotes not some minor pinprick, but deep and serious trouble. When life is difficult, don't give up hope — be patient and keep on praying, looking to God for a way to deal with the problems.

Rejoicing in Hope

As believers we are to be constantly rejoicing in the hope that we have. Hope refers to that glorious future expectancy which is guaranteed because God said it. As we look to the future we can do so with confident and rejoicing expectancy. The future is as bright as the promises of God. The coming of the Lord Jesus is a sure thing! Every child of God has a very bright future, and this ought to bring great rejoicing to our hearts. Romans chapter 8 has much to say about our future expectancy!

The person who does not look at what can be seen but eagerly waits for what cannot be seen is the one who rejoices in hope.

— Origen

Patient in Tribulation

The word "patient" carries the idea of staying under the trials of life, persevering, bearing up under, staying with it, "hanging in there", not giving up but keep going on in spite of all the difficulties and obstacles and problems and pressures! In 1Th1:3 we learn that hope produces patience. It's because of hope that we can endure and continue on in the midst of tribulation and pressure. Hope looks beyond the present trial and lays hold of the promises of God. "Continuing steadfastly" means adhering to, persisting in. The believer must give himself to prayer and be strong in prayer. Prayer demands effort and persistence. It is not easy to pray and it is not easy to stay with it (see the other usages of this verb in Acts 1:14; 2:42; 6:4; Col. 4:2).

Devoted to Prayer

In Rom12:12, he states that we display true love when we are rejoicing in hope, persevering in tribulation, devoted to prayer. There is a logical progression of thought here. Rejoicing in the certain hope of God's promises leads to persevering through tribulation, and one advantage in tribulation is that tribulation makes it easier to pray! Nothing will make you love a person so much as praying for him or her.

The person who prays best is the person who loves best. Are you having a struggle loving another brother or sister in Christ? Today, will you begin praying for him or her? The Lord can often resolve the issues as you turn to Him in prayer.

St Paul exhorted the Ephesian believers to see prayer as a weapon to use in fighting spiritual battles (Eph6:18). As we go through the day, prayer should be our first response to every fearful situation, every anxious thought, and every undesired task that God commands. A lack of prayer will cause us to depend on ourselves instead of depending on God's grace. Unceasing prayer is, in essence, continual dependence upon and communion with the Father.

For Christians, prayer should be like breathing. You do not have to think to breathe because the atmosphere exerts pressure on your lungs and essentially forces you to breathe. That is why it is more difficult to hold your breath than it is to breathe. Similarly, when we are born into the family of God, we enter into a spiritual atmosphere where God's presence and grace exert pressure, or influence, on our lives. Prayer is the normal response to that pressure. As believers, we have all entered the divine atmosphere to breathe the air of prayer.

"Devoted" means dedicated for a task, appointed for it. What's remarkable about this word is that five of the ten New Testament uses apply to prayer. Besides Rom12:12 there are:

Acts1:14 (after the ascension of Our Lord Jesus while the disciples were waiting in Jerusalem for the outpouring of the Spirit), "These all with one mind were continually devoting themselves to prayer, along with the women, and Mary the mother of Jesus, and with His brothers."

Acts2:42 (Of the early converts in Jerusalem), "They were continually devoting themselves to the apostles' teaching and to fellowship, to the breaking of bread and to prayer."

Acts6:4 (The apostles say), "But we will devote ourselves to prayer and to the ministry of the word."

Col 4:2 (St Paul says to all of us), "Devote yourselves to prayer, keeping alert in it with an attitude of thanksgiving."

So we may say from the New Testament scriptures that the normal Christian life is a life devoted to prayer. And so you should ask, "Am I devoted to prayer?"

It does not mean that prayer is all you do — any more than being devoted to a wife means all the husband does is hang out with his wife. But his devotion to her affects everything in his life and causes him to give himself to her in many different ways. So being devoted to prayer doesn't mean that all you do is pray although St Paul does say, "pray without ceasing," 1Th5:17. It means that there will be a pattern of praying that looks like devotion to prayer. It won't be the same for everyone. But it will be something significant. Being devoted to prayer looks different from not being devoted to prayer. And God knows the difference. He will call us to account: have we been devoted to prayer? Is there a pattern of praying in your life that can fairly be called "being devoted to prayer"?

Briefly, there are three reasons to why we should be devoted to prayer.

• The Bible tells us to pray and we should do what God says. This text, along with many other says, "Be devoted to prayer." If we are not, we are disobedient to the scriptures. That is foolish and dangerous.

• The needs in your own life, and in your family, and in this church and other churches, and in the cause of world missions, and in our culture at large are huge and desperate. In many cases heaven and hell hang in the balance, faith or unbelief, life and death. Remember St Paul's grief and anguish for his perishing kinsmen in Rom9:2, and remember that in Rom10:1 he prays for them earnestly, "Brothers, my heart's desire and prayer to God for them is that they may be saved." Salvation hangs in the balance when we pray.

• A third reason to pray is that God acts when we pray. And God can do more in five seconds than we can do in five years. Being devoted to prayer will mean that what you say in your times of prayer will often be free and unstructured, and often be formed and structured. If you are only free in your prayers, you will probably become shallow and trite. If you are only formed in your prayers, you will probably become mechanical and hollow. Both ways of praying are important. Not either/or, but both/ and.

By free I mean you will regularly feel like pouring out your soul to God and you will do it. You will not want any script or guidelines or lists or books. You will have so many needs that they tumble out freely without any pre-set form. This is good. Without this it is doubtful that we have any true relation with Christ at all. Can you really imagine a marriage or friendship where all the communication read from lists or books, or spoken only in memorized texts? That would be artificial in the extreme. Being devoted to prayer will mean that you will regularly pray alone and regularly pray in the assembly of other Christians.

Being devoted to prayer will mean that you come to God in prayer often desperate and often delighted. This simply means that prayer is a place for meeting God with your deepest heartaches and fears and prayer is a place for meeting God with your highest joys and thanks. The pillow you use for your elbows when you kneel daily before the Father, will be a tear-stained pillow. And yet, because God is a prayer-hearing God, you will say with the apostle St Paul, "sorrowful yet always rejoicing" (2Co6:10). And often that joy will overwhelm the burdens of this fallen world — as it should — and make you want to leap for joy. The Father wants to meet you at those times too. Be devoted to prayer in desperation and in delight — in fasting and feasting. Not either/or, but both/and.

If you are devoted to prayer you will explode regularly with prayers of praise and thanks and need and they will not last more than a few seconds. And if you are devoted to prayer you will have times when you linger for a long time in prayer to the Lord.

If we are devoted to prayer we will pray spontaneously through the day — without ceasing as St Paul says — a constant spirit of communion with Christ, walking by the Spirit and knowing Him as a continual personal presence in your life. No plan will govern when you speak to Him. It will happen dozens of time in the day. This is normal and good. This is being devoted to prayer.

To Be devoted to prayer is to be constant in it; to be faithful in it. Why? God commands us to; the needs are great and eternity hangs in the balance; and God hears and does more in five seconds that we can do in five years.

Attending to The Needs of the Saints

There is a connection between Rom12:12 and Rom12:13. Times of tribulation demand a spirit of generosity and hospitality when others are in need. Share with God's people who are in need. Practice hospitality (Rom12:13). Our possessions, like other gifts, should be used to serve others. Our care and concern will demonstrate itself in practical deeds done for others, either going to them (distributing to the needs of the saints) or inviting them to come to you (given to hospitality). The Greek word for hospitality is literally translated, "love for strangers"; and given is a strong word, meaning to "pursue" people with hospitality. Even if we don't own a home, we can be hospitable. At church, for example, we can be hospitable by welcoming others, being easy to approach and willing to help.

There are believers who have genuine needs which I am able to meet. Am I sensitive to the needs of other believers? Am I willing to give of myself, my time, my money, etc. to meet these needs in a Christ-honouring way?

It is not just guests that St Paul calls saints but also those who are in any kind of need.

— St Theodoret

To sum up, Rom12:9-13 contains a series of brief instructions on living like a Christian with others. We should see in this, as much as anything, a call to simple good manners among Christians. If we are called to warm relations and good manners, the church is also called to hard work: not lagging in diligence, fervent in spirit, serving the Lord; the church is no place for laziness. We are commanded to do all these things with an eye towards heaven. This is how we fulfil the command for hope, patience and steadfast character spoken of. Difficult times do not excuse from abandoning any of these things, nor do they excuse a lack of love in the body of Christ or a lack of willingness to do His work. For St Paul, there was no point in talking about love among God's people without the concrete demonstration of simply doing whatever we can to help each other.

GENERAL CHRISTIAN PRECEPTS

"Bless those who persecute you; bless and do not curse. Rejoice with those who rejoice, and weep with those who weep. Be of the same mind toward one another. Do not set your mind on high things, but associate with the humble. Do not be wise in your own opinion. Repay no one evil for evil. Have regard for good things in the sight of all men. If it is possible, as much as depends on you, live peaceably with all men. Beloved, do not avenge yourselves, but rather give place to wrath; for it is written, 'Vengeance is Mine, I will repay,' says the Lord. Therefore, 'If your enemy is hungry, feed him; if he is thirsty, give him a drink; for in so doing you will heap coals of fire on his head.' Do not be overcome by evil, but overcome evil with good," Rom 12:14-21.

In Rom12:14-21, St Paul instructs us how to get along with people both inside and outside the church. In the church, we are fellow members of the same body. God has united us with each other in a wonderful way. "The members should have the same care one for another. And whether one member suffer, all the members suffer with it; or one member be honoured, all the members rejoice with it" (1Co12:25-26). We are to feel for one another, entering into their joys and into their sorrows. Since I am a member of the same body as you are, your joys are my joys and your tears are my tears. I am not independent, but rather I am connected with every other member of the body. I need them and they need me. Sometimes it is more difficult to rejoice with a person than to weep with a person. This is because of pride, jealousy, envy, etc.

Virtually all the commands in Rom12:14-21 assume that something deeper has happened. All these commands are rooted in freedom from self-preoccupation and self-infatuation and self-exaltation. And, much more than that — though that is crucial — they are rooted in Christ-preoccupation and Christ-infatuation and Christ-exaltation as a result of the gift of faith (Rom12:3).

HOW CHRISTIANS RELATE TO NON-CHRISTIANS

"Bless those who persecute you; bless and do not curse. Rejoice with those who rejoice, and weep with those who weep," Rom 12:14-15

God the Father planned to rescue us from sin and hell before the foundation of the world. God the Son purchased our forgiveness and transformation by His blood on the Cross. God the Spirit overcame all our self-preoccupation and self-infatuation and self-exaltation and opened our eyes to see the beauty of Christ as our all. Now in this condition we meet today three kinds of people: those who persecute us, those who rejoice, and those who weep. St Paul tells us, with God's authority, how to treat them. Here is the way a person lives for whom Christ is all and for whom self is dethroned. "Bless those who persecute you; bless and do not curse them. Rejoice with those who rejoice, weep with those who weep," Rom12:14-15.

Bless and Don't Curse

The Greek word for "bless" means "to speak well of a person". This requires incredible self-control and grace. We are not to have a hateful attitude towards anyone; not even those who persecute us. Our Lord Jesus spoke of this same heart in Mt5:46, "For if you love those who love you, what reward have you? Do not even the tax collectors do the same?" We are to receive grace, but we are to also give it. We are to walk in the way Jesus walked.

How can the Scriptures which forbid us to curse, contain so many curses themselves? Those curses are not spoken by a person who desires their fulfilment but merely foretell the fact. They do not want this to befall sinners, but because they will doubtless come to pass these curses proved to be prophecies.

– St Caesarius of Arles

"Curse": This is the natural reaction toward our enemies but it is not the Christian reaction. St Paul is instructing us not to pronounce judgment upon people who chase after and pursue believers with a hostile intent to harm and to hurt. Remember how the book of Deuteronomy speaks of the blessings and the curses. Actually St Paul is here repeating the teaching of Christ Himself (Mt5:44). Do not curse! Give a blessing where a curse is deserved. Isn't that what Jesus did for us? It is the world's way to give back what we are given. If someone hates us, we hate them back. If someone hurts us, we pay back in kind. Yet, when we do that, our enemies defeat us. We don't win a victory, but we lose. We become the very thing that we hate.

How radical this behaviour is! It does not just say: Don't retaliate. You might use your willpower to do that. You might have all kinds of hateful and resentful and vengeful and also prudential motives for not striking back. But the point is not only behaviour. The point is your heart, and you can see it in the words, "Bless those who persecute you. Bless and do not curse them." This is a partial quotation of Jesus' words in Lk6:28 where Jesus says, "Bless those who curse you, pray for those who abuse you." The word "pray" shows that behaviour is not the only issue. Prayer is the expression to God of what you long for. So blessing someone is not just the way you treat him. It includes the longings that you have for someone. And Jesus says they are to be longings for good, not longings for a curse. That's what "bless" means. Bless them and pray for them. Pray for what? Their good — now and forever. And the greatest good is seeing and savouring and showing Christ without end.

Pray for Those Who Hurt You

How do we pray for those who purposefully, knowingly use and abuse us? How do we act like sons and daughters of our Father in heaven? Here are five ways:

• Pray that God would forgive them. Although it's vital that you forgive your persecutors, we walk the way Jesus walked when we pray for God to forgive our enemies. Both Jesus and Stephen, while they were being persecuted by enemies of the Gospel, prayed, "Father, forgive them, for they know not what they do" (Lk23:34; Acts7:60). If you want to be more Christ-like, pray like Christ prayed when He was persecuted.

• Pray for God to give them a spirit of wisdom and revelation in the knowledge of Jesus. Obviously, your persecutors need a greater revelation of Jesus, because the more we truly know Christ, the less we'll allow the devil to influence our thoughts, words and deeds. Pray "that the God of our Lord Jesus Christ, the Father of glory, may give to (them) the spirit of wisdom and revelation in the knowledge of Him, the eyes of (their) understanding being enlightened; that (they) may know what is the hope of His calling, what are the riches of the glory of His inheritance in the saints, and what is the exceeding greatness of His power toward us who believe, according to the working of His mighty power," Eph1:17-19.

• Pray for God to root them and ground them in love. We know that love is kind (1Co13:4) but whoever slanders is a fool (Pr10:18). The Bible doesn't have anything good to say about fools, but God still loves them — and if they were rooted and grounded in the love of God, they would not gossip, slander or persecute people. Pray that they, "being rooted and grounded in love, may be able to comprehend with all the saints what is the width and length and depth and height — to know the love of Christ which passes knowledge; that (they) may be filled with all the fullness of God," Eph3:17-19.

• Pray for God's love to abound in them. You can't walk out the Beatitudes without abounding in love. Pray that your persecutor's love "may abound still more and more in knowledge and all discernment, that (they) may approve the things that are excellent, that (they) may be sincere and without offense till the day of Christ, being filled with the fruits of righteousness which are by Jesus

Christ, to the glory and praise of God," Php1:9-11.

• **Pray for God to show them His will.** Once your persecutor is rooted and grounded in love and understands God's will, they will be more likely to repent. Pray that they "may be filled with the knowledge of His will in all wisdom and spiritual understanding; that (they) may walk worthy of the Lord, fully pleasing Him, being fruitful in every good work and increasing in the knowledge of God," Col 1:9-10.

Beyond that, intercede as the Holy Spirit leads you until you feel a release in your spirit. And remember, St Paul admonishes us to "bless those who persecute you; bless and do not curse," Rom12:14. At its root, to bless means to speak well of, and to curse means to speak ill of. So don't respond to your persecutors by running all over town telling people what they did to you. If you do, you'll be guilty of gossip, slander and cursing your enemy. Move in the opposite spirit. If you respond God's way, you'll be blessed.

As for your enemy, well, he's likely to be blessed with some conviction from the Holy Spirit, and your prayers pave the way for you both to grow in the character of Christ as you guard your heart from bitterness.

Show Sympathy

"Bless those who persecute you; bless and do not curse. Rejoice with those who rejoice, and weep with those who weep," Rom12:14-15. Taking the two verses together immediately raises the question what they have to do with each other. Anything? More than you may think. For example, what would be one reason that you wouldn't weep with those who weep? One reason would be that you are glad they are weeping. In other words, you were angry at them for the way they treated you, and then something bad happened to them and you are glad. Does that have anything to do with verse 14: Don't curse those who persecute you. Don't want them to be cursed. Don't be glad when they weep. Bless them. So it looks as if there may be a very close connection between verses 14 and 15.

To be haughty is pride, which is how the devil fell... Solomon says, 'God resists the proud,' Pr3:34. Put pride aside and make other people's cares your own so that you might be acceptable to God.

— St Ambrosiaster

We can show sympathy when believers and unbelievers are hurting, but it is often another thing when we are called to rejoice in the blessings of others. We are to look for opportunities to love. If we were to share in the lives of others by experiencing their joy and feeling their grief, all kinds of walls would come crashing down. So the Christian life is radical. It cuts to the root of who we are and what we long for. This kind of radical behaviour comes from faith in Christ and it means that Christ is all-sufficient. It comes from not thinking of ourselves more highly than we ought to think, but thinking with sober judgment each according to the measure of faith that God has assigned (Rom12:3).

If we are going to be treated unjustly, and even hurt unjustly for Christ's sake, and yet bless our adversaries and pray for them, then our natural obsession with self-preoccupation and self-infatuation and self-exaltation must die. But that death will accomplish nothing by itself. It must be replaced by Christ-preoccupation and Christ-infatuation and Christ-exaltation. That's what faith is: beholding and embracing the all-satisfying treasure of Christ.

This looking to Christ motivates in three ways us to

bless our adversaries and make us tender-hearted to those who weep and rejoice. First, the Christ that faith beholds and embraces blessed those who cursed Him. As He hung on the Cross He said, "Father, forgive them, for they know not what they do," Lk23:34. Since faith savours everything it sees about Christ, it savours this too. If you see and savour mercy in Christ, you will love being merciful.

Second, the Christ that faith beholds and embraces did not just bless His enemies in the abstract; He did this for me. "While we were still weak, at the right time Christ died for the ungodly," Rom5:6. You cannot rejoice that your life hangs totally on the undeserved mercy of being blessed by Christ when you were His enemy, and then turn around and curse those who persecute you.

Third, the Christ that faith beholds and embraces has made our future absolutely secure forever, by dying for us and rising again. Therefore, our persecutors cannot destroy us, and we do not need to have the last word on earth. God will. "Do not fear those who kill the body but cannot kill the soul. Rather fear him who can destroy both soul and body in hell. Are not two sparrows sold for a penny? And not one of them will fall to the ground apart from your Father. But even the hairs of your head are all numbered. Fear not, therefore; you are of more value than many sparrows," Mt10:28-31.

The root of radical, Christ-like love is death to self and invincible delight in the person, the performance, and the promises of Christ. If you struggle with feelings of bitterness and revenge, go deeper with Christ, until you know Him and love Him the way He really is.

Have The Same Mind-Set

Rejoice with those who rejoice, and weep with those who weep is how we can fulfil the command to be of the same mind toward one another. It is a simple command to be considerate of the feelings of others instead of waiting for them to be considerate of your feelings. By the way, one of the practical ways we can fulfil this command is to attend weddings and funerals.

"Be of the same mind toward one another. Do not set your mind on high things, but associate with the humble. Do not be wise in your own opinion," Rom 12:15-16

With believers, "Be of the same mind" means think the same thing, be in agreement, live in harmony, be harmonious. We must not be out of harmony with the body (think of the human body and what it would be like if one leg wanted to go north and the other leg wanted to go south or if one eye wanted to look to the left and the other to the right (Compare Php4:2 and 2Co13:11). Believers need to agree together, to cherish the same views, to be unanimous. There must be no discord or disagreement. "Who is in favour of glorifying God?" Everyone agrees and says, "Amen!" "Who believes that pleasing Christ is top priority?" Everyone is unanimous and says, "Amen!" "Who wants to follow Christ and fight the good fight of faith?" Everyone steps forward and says, "I Do!" "Who hates sin and error?" Everyone answers, "We all do!" This is the kind of agreement that needs to exist among believers. We must not pursue different ends and aims. If we hold the same view as God does, then we will agree with each other.

When St Paul is calling all believers to a common mindset, he is not suggesting that we must all think in just the same way or that we must think exactly the same thing about every issue. Instead, we are to agree to disagree agreeably over non-essentials. In doing so we demonstrate the love, unity, and sacrifice that can only be found in Christ.

Associate with the Humble

St Paul commands us not to be haughty in mind. This is a warning against prideful ambition (to seek high things such as honour and riches, position and power, to be aspiring). Do not aspire after high things (Ps131:1). Rather, to associate with the lowly. The word translated "lowly" refers to those first-century Christians who could boast of little in the way of worldly goods or social position. Grammatically this can mean one of two things: 1) lowly men (masculine); 2) lowly things (neuter). The masculine would mean this: Associate with humble folk, don't consider such people as beneath you (we have the example of Christ who had friends among the publicans and sinners and outcasts and poor, etc.). The neuter would mean this: Accommodate yourself to humble ways, yield or submit to lowly things, conditions, employments, in contrast to high things which were just mentioned.

Avoid Self-Conceit

The command, "Do not be wise in your own estimation" is a warning against being conceited (having a very high opinion of yourself) in all your dealings. Don't be wise in your own estimation (in your own eyes; Pr3:7 and Is5:21) even with unbelievers. It also implies that we need to recognize that often the socially "lower" Christian has much more to give than the rich Christian. Indeed, all Christians have something to share with other Christians; and all Christians have things to learn from other Christians. We need to get over ourselves! We need to see our fellow believers accurately and biblically. We need to exercise humility (Rom12:12:3, 10b). If we're humble, we'll never look down on anyone. We can only look up to them. May we begin to regard others as more important than ourselves (Php2:3). May we ensure that our Christian relationships are healthy and whole. Love without action is not love.

In refusing to set our mind on high things and associating with the humble, we are simply imitating Jesus; do not be wise in your own opinion reminds us of how far we still have to go in actually being like Jesus.

REPAY NO ONE EVIL FOR EVIL

"Repay no one evil for evil. Have regard of good things in the sight of all men. If it be possible, as much as depends on you, live peaceably with all men," Rom12:17-18

"Evil for evil" means "evil in return for evil". "Recompense or repay" means to give back, thus to render, to reward, to pay back someone for the evil they have done (someone punches you in the nose and you give back the same treatment to him). This attitude is expressed in this way, "I'm going to pay you back for that! I'm going to get even! You're not going to get away with that! You're going to pay for this!" Instead of the golden rule we have the dirty rule: do unto others just as they have done unto you or worse! When is it proper to return evil for evil? From the Sermon on the Mount (Mt5:44) to the end of the New Testament, the answer is, "Never!" Don't give the person what he may deserve (1Th5:15 and 1Pt3:9). How thankful we each need to be that God does not give us what we deserve (Ps103:10; Ps130:3-4).

What about the Old Testament teaching of "eye for eye, tooth for tooth" (Ex21:24) etc.? This means that the punishment should fit the crime, and this is a true and valid principle of justice. A person should get just what he deserves. See for example, Gn9:6 (life for life). Is it true that the Old Testament teaches a doctrine of retaliation whereas the New Testament teaches a doctrine of non-retaliation? Pr20:22 and Pr25:21-22 are both from the Old Testament, and both teach non-retaliation. Also Rom13:1-4 is from the New Testament and this passage clearly teaches that evil-doers should be punished, and that God does this through governments, etc.

In Romans 12 St Paul is not saying that evil men should not be punished. His main point, as we shall see, is that the believer should let God the Perfect Judge take care of wrong and injustices in His way and in His time (Rom12:19 for example). In other words, carefully and deliberately think through how you will respond if someone does something to you or one of your family members. If you fail to do so, you will respond according to your fleshly impulses. Conflict, however, ought to be in spite of you not because of you. Hence, it is critical to think carefully of how you should respond in every situation so that even unbelievers observe your life and glorify God. In other words, do not harbour grudges, and be sensitive to social values.

Praise-Worthy Behaviour

"Have regard for good things in the sight of all men". This verse is a quote from Pr3:4 in the LXX and compares 2Co8:21. The NIV translates it this way: "be careful to do what is right and good in the sight of everybody." We have a testimony. People are watching and looking. They know how a Christian should act. They will watch and see whether or not we retaliate as the world does, whether or not we try to "get even". An important verse which sheds much light on Rom12:17 is 1Th5:15.

Today we are living in a lawsuit infatuated society whose motto seems to be "sue or be sued!" The emphasis is on how much I can get out of the other person for my own personal benefit. This is the opposite of the principles of love as set forth in this chapter. Love always asks, "How much can I give to this person even if it means personal loss and sacrifice?" In such a mixed up society, believers whose hearts are filled with the love of Christ should shine very brightly! Our job is not to use and abuse others for our own personal gain!

"Have regard for good things in the sight of all men" is a way to live out the idea of praising what is good; people should be able to see what is good and what is not, based on our conduct. It has many practical applications. It touches how we dress and act, the way we treat others in public, it involves things like common courtesy, honesty at work, having a cheerful heart, being a team player, not being a troublemaker, a grump, a whiner, a constant complainer, or a hypochondriac. The principle is: Live in such a way that no one can make an honest accusation against you. Live so that if they are going to accuse you, they have to tell a lie to do it.

Pursue Peace with All People

"Live peaceably" means "be at peace, live at peace". "Live peaceably with all men" reminds us that though we are in contrast to the world, we do not seek out contention. St Paul goes a step further when he says, "If possible, so far as it depends on you, be at peace with all men." Notice the conditional nature of this verse. The phrases "if possible" and "so far as it depends on you" reveal that you can't force others to do what is right. Once you have done everything within your power to resolve a conflict, you have fulfilled your responsibility to God. Now, if circumstances change and there seems to be a new opportunity for peace with an enemy, you should pursue it. Peace is a two-way street. We must do our part to live peaceably, but we have no control over the other's conduct. I may have a snowball and the other person has one. I can choose not to throw mine at him but I can't control what he does with his. St Paul's point is this: The disturbance to the peace should never be initiated by the Christian. The believer should never be the one to break the peace. The believer is told to pursue peace (run after it: Rom14:19; 2Ti2:22; Heb12:14 and 1Pt3:11).

The apostle here gives a very balanced command because he knows perfectly well that peace depends on both parties, and the other party may as well be hostile and block peace. What he asks is that our mind should be ready for peace and that the blame for any discord should lie with the other side and not with us.

— Origen

In the meantime, you should not waste time, energy, and resources with a person who refuses to be reconciled. Therefore, don't blame yourself. Some people are just antagonistic. Some conflicts require mediation from a mature Christian. You can't control other people or how they respond to you. But you can create an environment that either makes it more or less likely for them to blow up in your face.

The principle is: Be a peacemaker to the point that, if someone makes trouble for you, no one can legitimately blame you. Trust God to change the other person. He prepares and softens hearts. Often it takes a great deal of prayer and many months or years before a person is willing to reconcile. We must be patient and wait on God. Get the help of a third party.

"Beloved, do not avenge yourselves, but rather give place to wrath: for it is written, 'Vengeance is mine; I will repay', says the Lord. Therefore, if your enemy is hungry, feed him; if he is thirsty, give him a drink: for in so doing you shall heap coals of fire on his head. Do not be overcome by evil, but overcome evil with good," Rom12:19-21, quoting Dt32:35; Pr25:21, 22

Don't Avenge Yourself

There are no exceptions. Revenge and retaliation are forever ruled out for the believer in Christ. Most people want revenge, but that is a destructive approach. Don't get your revenge! St Paul gives us three reasons for ruling out all attempts at revenge. First, vengeance is perfect and righteous judgement, which only God is capable of carrying out. St Paul wants you to give God His job description back. "Give place unto (the) wrath": give the wrath of God an opportunity to work out its purpose. Step aside and leave the matter to God and leave the matter with God. Yield and hand the person over to God's wrath which will take care of it at the right time and in the right way. Do not give the devil a chance or opportunity to exert his influence, don't give him an opening (Eph4:27).

God wants an opportunity to take care of wrongs done to His children, and it is His right to do so. God is the avenger of wrath! God is much more angry at sin than we are! He is also much more long suffering than we are!

God will straighten things out. The wicked will not get away with anything. I do not need to get even, but God will. By refusing to take revenge, you are leaving room for God to exercise His wrath. The wrath of God is likely both temporal and eternal in this context.

Second, there is a better way to get even (Rom12:20). St Paul quotes Dt32:35 to serve as a reminder that no one can avenge you quite like God. Therefore, if you want Him to avenge you, step out of His way. If you want to avenge yourself, God will remove His hand from your situation. The most fundamental reason not to take revenge is that by our clumsiness we may block God's work in another person's life. We just want to get even, but God wants to bring that person to a place of repentance and reconciliation. God has a better view than we do and He has a higher goal. Vengeance is His specialty.

> If we do not do what God teaches, He will show us contempt. But if we give revenge over to God it benefits us in two ways: it overcomes our anger and tends toward our perfection and justification in God's sight.
>
> — St Ambrosiaster

It might help to define who the "enemy" is in this verse. The "enemy" is almost always a friend, a colleague or a family member who has hurt me in some way. My enemy by definition will almost always be someone close to me. An enemy is any person God uses to reveal my weaknesses. An enemy is like a chisel God uses to chip away at the rough spots in my life. That's why if you are married, your husband or your wife will be your enemy about half the time. No one knows your weaknesses like your spouse. They know hidden blemishes, secret sins, bad habits, that the rest of the world never sees. But they know it because they live with you every day. That's why you have to feed your enemy. You can't let your wife or your husband starve to death. It wouldn't look good in the newspaper. That's why you have to give your boss or your teacher or that obnoxious person in the next office something to drink. These are people who are close to you, and because they are close to you, God is using them to expose the weak areas of your life. The one who trusts in God will not think it necessary to avenge themselves; they will leave the issue of vengeance to God, and give place to wrath - giving no place to their own wrath, and a wide place to God's wrath.

> "If you are suffering from a bad man's injustice, forgive him, lest there be two bad men."
> — St Augustine

In the Kingdom of God, the way to be free from our enemies is not to destroy them or repay in kind. It is to forgive them. An unforgiven enemy will always have a hold on us in some way or another. If we forgive, we are free. Jesus died for us while we were yet God's enemies (Rom5:12). He took the wrath we deserved upon Himself and gave us not the blessings we deserve but the blessings He Himself has with the Father (Eph1:3). Some say that the Grace of the new covenant makes no demands upon those who receive it. This is true, but at the same time Grace compels us to give to others what we have been given. We are to give others and even our enemies the opposite of what they deserve, a blessing and not a curse.

Does this mean that you are called to be a doormat? No, you are not called to be a doormat; you are called to be an elevator. You are to lift people up into the presence of God by graciously giving your enemy food and drink in his or her time of need. St Paul says, in so doing "you will heap burning coals on his head." What would qualify as "hot coals?" A kind word, a phone call, a brief note, a flower, a meal, a small gift, a letter of recommendation, running an errand, offering a ride, helping them complete a project, rewriting their report, stepping in to save a project that was failing, putting in a good word with their superiors, helping them clean the classroom, going bowling with them. The list is endless, because "hot coals" refers to any act of kindness you do for an enemy. Your only limit is your creativity.

The burning coals is a figure of God's judgment that will come on your enemy if he or she persists in antagonism. The figure of "coals of fire" in the Old Testament consistently refers to God's anger and judgment (2Sam22:9, 13;

Ps11:6; 18:13; 140:9-10; Pr25:21-22). Thus the meaning appears to be that you can return good for evil with the assurance that God will eventually punish your enemy, if you don't win him or her by your lovingkindness.

Third, revenge destroys you but good overcomes evil. "Do not be overcome by evil, but overcome evil with good," Rom12:21. When St Paul says, "Do not be overcome with evil," what he means is, "Don't let revenge destroy your life." So many times we look at life as a kind of competition. "He hit me so I had to hit him back." "Sure, I said some awful things to him, but he said them to me first." This happens in marriage all the time. We play a game of tit for tat. You hurt me so now I'm going to hurt you. You cheated on me, so now it's okay if I cheat on you. You slapped me, so I can slap you back. You raised your voice, so now I'm going to raise mine just one decibel louder than yours. And on it goes. If we're Christians, we may even use the Bible to support that. You know, the part about an eye for an eye, a tooth for a tooth. It's called evening the score.

> It is the nature of evil to increase and grow by similar acts, rather like adding fire to fire.
>
> — Origen

Getting even doesn't work. What happens when you try to get even? You unleash this whole cycle of retribution and violence. It never ends because someone else always wants to get the last word. There is a very practical reason behind St Paul's advice. You may win the battle, you may even get the last word or strike the last blow, but in the end, you've destroyed your own spiritual life. In the process of hurting another person, you've hurt yourself too. Anger has done its dirty work on the inside. You seethe with malice, rage, hurtful feelings, and horrible thoughts that keep you up late at night. That's one reason why many people are sick today. They aren't sick because of some bug or strange virus. No, their soul is sick and as a result their body is sick. The list is long, but it includes high blood pressure, heart problems, back problems, tension headaches, nightmares, ulcers, stomach problems, weight problems, blurred vision, a stiff neck, and insomnia.

As long as you try to get even, you're still living in the past. It may have happened years ago, but you're still stewing about your divorce or how unfairly your boss treated you, or how your children disappointed you. The only way to get free of your past is to let it go once and for all.

"Do not be overcome by evil, but overcome evil with good," Rom 12: 21

Don't Be Overcome by Evil

So what does St Paul mean when he says, "Do not be overcome by evil, but overcome evil with good"? In the context, coming right after saying be good to your enemy, he means "Don't let your enemy's hostility produce hostility in you. But let your love triumph over his hostility." Don't be overcome by evil means. Don't be overcome by his evil. Don't let another person's evil make you evil. Oh, how crucial that is.

When you let your adversary make you evil he is the victor. If you let a person's sin govern your emotions so that your sinful anger or your misery or your depression is owing to their evil, then you are being overcome by evil. And St Paul says, You don't have to be overcome that way. St Paul is addressing here the whole victim mentality of our day — people who feel or do evil things and then blame it on someone else's evil. They let themselves be overcome by someone else's evil so that they now do evil also. And then they blame the other person.

But St Paul says, "Don't be overcome by evil." Don't let another person's evil provoke you to evil thoughts or evil attitudes or evil deeds. Don't give them that kind of power. You don't have to. Christ is your king. Christ is your leader, your champion, your treasure. Christ governs your life, not those who do evil. When someone does evil to you, you should say, "You are not my Lord. I will not be controlled by you. I will not have my attitudes and thoughts and actions dictated by your evil. Christ is my Lord. Christ dictates my attitudes and thoughts and actions.

Oh how different this is than the way most people react. We let our emotions and our thoughts and our actions be reflexes to what people say and do to us. And the corollary is that we can then blame them for our evil—our anger, our bitterness, our discouragement, our depression, our vengeance. But Paul says, No. When Christians encounter evil, they don't merely respond to evil, they respond to Christ who deals with the evil. He died for it, or he will punish it in hell. Christ is the dominant reality in our lives, not other people's evil. Therefore, do not be overcome by evil. Do not be governed by it. Do not let your enemy's hostility make you hostile.

Overcome Evil with Good

"Overcome evil with good." This is the bottom line. Although we live in a world where evil seems to win out, that's only a temporary situation. How did Jesus survive the most awful day in human history? How could He stand there and let Himself be accused of crimes He didn't commit? Why didn't He strike back? Why didn't He fight for His rights? The answer is "He entrusted Himself to Him who judges justly." He believed that God was a God of justice, therefore He didn't have to say a word in His own defence. He knew that God would take care of Him in the end. And He did. On Friday He was crucified. On Sunday He rose from the dead.

Suppose you were at a picnic and someone intentionally throws a football at you from close range, hits you hard on the head with it and then throws dirt in your face and spits at you. You could take some red-hot burning charcoals and while he is not looking pile them up on his head. Do you think he would like this? Of course not! That would be the worst kind of treatment you could give a person! What could be worse than that? That would be unbearable. That would really hurt!

God is saying this: If you want to get back at your enemy, then do good to him! That would be unbearable treatment. That would be the most effective thing you could do. It would be killing people with kindness; avenging them with virtue, destroying them with deeds of love and persecuting them with peace. "The coals of fire" symbolize the burning pangs of shame and contrition resulting from the unexpected kindness received. The wronged person's magnanimous behaviour, returning good for evil, has this effect.

Consider St Stephen. His enemies would probably have preferred that he throw stones at them instead of praying for them! That must have been painful to them! Next time you are wronged, try giving your enemy the "love treatment" and trust God to use it to work in their hearts. So the apostle says that the effect of doing good to an enemy would be to produce pain. But the pain will result from shame, remorse of conscience, a conviction of the evil of his conduct, and an apprehension of divine displeasure that may lead to repentance.

Our aim in loving our enemy is to bless him not curse him. "Bless those who persecute you; bless and do not curse them." Our first and most urgent longing for our enemies is that they be blessed — that they repent and that they trust Christ and that His ransom pay all their debts and give them salvation. Yes, that is the goal. Live so as to lead people into an enjoyment of the mercy of God.

Reflect Christ's Mercy

God calls us to be merciful — returning good for evil and treating our enemies better than they deserve — and all this to show people what God is like in His mercy and how He frees us from vengeance and greed and fear. If we become just like our enemies, they have won. The victory is in not becoming like them in an attempt to defeat them, but to overcome evil with good. Jesus said when a Roman soldier makes you carry his pack one mile, carry it two. The way you triumph in that situation is not to hate the

Roman soldier but to show astounding generosity instead. Could you imagine how a Roman soldier who received such kindness would feel? He would have a hard time hating the one who served him.

> *Don't let evil conquer you (have the victory over you), but go and conquer evil with good. Drown the evil in good.*

Evil is overcome only with good, which the Son of God Himself demonstrated on the Cross and which believers are called to emulate. If we respond to people in the way that Christ has treated us, then we will respond with good rather than evil. The surpassing greatness of the love of Our Lord Jesus Christ in us is that it can be extended to our enemies. Our Lord Jesus spoke all too accurately about "the time is coming that whoever kills you will think that he offers God service," Jn16:2. With this mind set, we will do good to our enemies, looking for the most practical ways we can to help them; this is the way we are not overcome by evil, but overcome evil with good. Jesus has shown us the way. Evil cannot be beaten by more evil — it can be conquered only by good.

To return evil for evil is natural; to return good for evil is supernatural. But this is how God's economy operates. Evil cannot overcome the Christian by doing us harm or even by killing us. Evil will only overcome us if it makes us use evil ourselves. Evil cannot be overcome by a stronger force of the same kind. If you feel that you can't live like He did, you're right. You can't be like Our Lord Jesus in your own strength. But if you depend on Him, He can give you the strength to keep quiet when you'd rather get even. May you and I refuse to be overcome by evil, but may we overcome evil with good.

Remember Our Lord Jesus' words, "all people will know that we are His disciples if we have love for one another," Jn13:35. We are the disciples of Him who died for His enemies. So now God says to His Son's disciples, "'If your enemy is hungry, feed him; if he is thirsty, give him something to drink; for by so doing you will heap burning coals on his head.' Do not be overcome by evil, but overcome evil with good." Love was very important to Our Lord Jesus; it compelled Him to give up His life for us! He wants us to imitate Him in how we love others.

So now we know that this is not a mere call from God to imitate Christ. It is a call to trust Christ for our own salvation, and then, in the hope and strength and joy and assurance of that salvation show it to others by the way we live. Identify those relationships where you need to grow in love — it may be a family member, a co-worker, a neighbour, or a person at church. Target specific people, not just everyone in general. Then commit to begin loving those people as Christ has commanded. Point them to Jesus as the only possible ransom for their sins — the only one who can pay their debt and overcome their evil with the good of His own death and resurrection.

Let God's Justice Triumph

"But overcome evil with good" in the context means "let your love triumph over your enemy's hostility." But what does that mean? Does it mean that, if you give him water when he is thirsty and food when he is hungry, he will always repent and become your friend? No. We know St Paul doesn't think that. Jesus's enemies do not all respond positively to His love for them. One thief on the cross repented and the other cursed. St Peter repented. Judas hanged himself. The centurion said, "This was the Son of God." The Pharisees said good riddance. The love of Christ does not produce repentance in everyone. And your love won't either. St Paul says, "If possible, so far as it depends on you, live peaceably with all," Rom12:18. In other words, you will do everything you should, and still some will not make peace.

But that's not the whole picture. Because we saw in verse 19, "Beloved, never avenge yourselves, but leave it to the wrath of God, for it is written, 'Vengeance is mine, I will repay, says the Lord.'" This means that when you love your enemy and they don't repent and receive the blessing of your love, evil does not triumph. God's justice triumphs. "I will repay says the Lord." You don't need to be the judge. God will. You don't need to win on earth. God will win for you in the last day. "Or do you presume on the riches of his kindness and forbearance and patience, not knowing that God's kindness is meant to lead you to repentance? But because of your hard and impenitent heart you are storing up wrath for yourself on the day of wrath when God's righteous judgment will be revealed," Rom2:4-5.

The result of God's love for His enemies when it is rejected is very much like coals of fire. This is the way God's love works for His enemies, and it is the way our love works for our enemies. Our aim is in verse 14: "Bless and do not curse." Pray for your enemies. Be like St Paul in Rom10:1, "My heart's desire and prayer to God for them is that they may be saved." Our desire is that they would repent and come to a knowledge of the truth. But if they don't, the very love that we are showing increases the weight of wrath on their head. The more of God's mercy that people reject, the more wrath they heap up upon themselves.

For this, we are willing to lay down our lives — that our enemies will be saved. Thousands of missionaries have done it. But what verse 20 is saying is this: If it looks like your love has failed, and instead of converting your enemy, your enemy kills you, be assured, you have overcome evil. It has not overcome you. God will have the last word, not your enemy. You will be vindicated in the resurrection of the just. For this, Christ died and rose again.

So what does "overcome evil with good" mean? It means either you triumph through the repentance of your enemy or you triumph through the judgment of your enemy. In other words, if you will love your enemy, and bless those who curse you (Rom12:14), and not return evil for evil (Rom12:17), and not avenge yourselves (Rom12:19), you will be the overcomer, the conqueror, the victor no matter how your enemy responds. Be strong, Christians. Don't be overcome by evil. Overcome evil with good.

In Rom12:17-21, St Paul teaches that the Christian response to being wronged is to do right toward your enemy, leaving all vengeance with God. Our aim must be (as St Paul's was; Php1:20) to exalt Christ in our bodies through selflessness or self-denial, whether by life or by death. Our desire should be that our enemy would come to know the same mercy and Grace that we found at the Cross. And so, rather than responding to the evil done against us with evil or with vengeance, we are commanded to respond with the radical love of Christ that overcomes evil with good. The world says, "Don't get mad; get even!" But our Lord says, "Love your enemies, do good to those who hate you," Lk6:27.

Jesus' words in the Sermon on the Mount were troubling and subversive in His day, and they still are in ours. His words should trouble our hearts. We should wrestle with them to find their meaning in our lives that we might walk in the way our Master did. He walked in grace all the way to the Cross.

It is not the believer's job to punish evildoers. This is God's job. He is the avenger of wrath. Vengeance belongs to Him. He will repay in His way and in His time. Romans 13 tells us that one of the ways that God punishes evildoers is through human government which He has ordained and established (Rom13:4).

I challenge you to spend some time this week meditating on Rom 12:10-21. Ask yourself repeatedly, "Do I 'abhor what is evil?' Am I enraged over pride, selfishness, favouritism, revenge, and other ungodly behaviours?" Then ask yourself, "Do I 'cling to what is good?' Am I enthralled with humility, selflessness, generosity, and servanthood?" Love without action is not love.